DEVELOPMENT
IN PRACTICE

Private Sector Development in Low-Income Countries

Private Sector Development in Low-Income Countries

THE WORLD BANK
WASHINGTON D.C.

The Development in Practice series publishes reviews of the World
Bank's activities in different regions and sectors. It lays particular
emphasis on the progress that is being made and on the policies and
practices that hold the most promise of success in the effort to reduce
poverty in the developing world.

This book is a product of the staff of the World Bank, and the judgments
made herein do not necessarily reflect the views of its Board of Executive
Directors or the countries they represent.

Photo credits: World Bank

ISBN 0-8213-3478-6

Contents

BOXES

Foreword

IN response to a request by the Deputies of the International Development Association, this report assesses the progress of private sector development in low-income countries, particularly in Sub-Saharan Africa, during the IDA 9 and IDA 10 periods (from 1987 onward). It identifies causes of uneven performance and outlines the main elements of a strategy—led by the private sector—for accelerated and shared growth to reduce poverty.

Private sector development contributes to poverty reduction in two ways. First, it enhances competitive forces and competitiveness, which produce growth and jobs. Second, through divestiture of activities that the private sector can do as well or better, it allows governments to reduce waste and gain the fiscal space needed for greater investments in the social sectors and infrastructure. Those investments are "income equalizers" that provide skills and services required by the private sector to compete in today's skill-based global economy.

Though pivotal, private sector development is only part of an overall strategy for sustainable development that embraces such other elements as health, education, infrastructure, and environmental protection. These topics are treated in other periodic and special reports, including "A Continent in Transition: Sub-Saharan Africa in the 1990s."

This report argues that for private sector development to promote accelerated growth, progress on the macroeconomic front has to be buttressed with structural and institutional reforms to:

- Improve business environments that remain harsh.
- Reduce the drain of public enterprises.
- Build robust financial systems.
- Increase the supply and quality of human resources and physical infrastructure.

In many countries, public enterprise losses are on the order of 8–12 percent of GDP. They absorb most domestic savings in Sub-Saharan Africa and are 2–3 times government spending on health and education. But for these losses, real per capita GDP growth in reforming African countries would have been 3–4 percent a year instead of only 1 percent. Public sector inefficiencies have limited job growth and in the process deprived a large part of the population of the benefits of reforms—undermining the political support for difficult structural changes needed to compete in a global economy.

This report calls for faster and more widely shared growth. How? By shifting from preserving jobs in a public sector that has failed to generate productive employment to creating jobs in a vibrant private sector. Only with such a shift will it be possible to absorb new workers, the unemployed, and those losing employment as a result of public enterprise and civil service restructuring. But it will require a fundamental change in the role of government—from owner and operator to policymaker and regulator that works closely with the private sector to develop a competitive, outward-looking economy. Success will depend on a major sustained effort to develop agile, competent, and respected public institutions.

Specifically, the strategy requires that low-income countries:

- Sustain sound macroeconomic management to avoid the stop-go policies that have undermined private sector confidence.
- Establish a more favorable business environment to promote competition and reduce risk and the high cost of doing business, which have especially stunted the growth of firms in the informal sector and small and medium-size enterprises. This means pressing ahead on an array of policy, legal, regulatory, and institutional reforms in partnership with business and labor.
- Go farther and faster on public sector reform by privatizing the utilities and the largest enterprises—and by liquidating major loss-makers. Employing only a small fraction of the labor force, these enterprises preempt a large part of government expenditures and account for a large part of the losses of the banking system. Failure to deal with these losses threatens the reform program and diverts resources from pressing social needs.
- Accelerate financial reform by restructuring and privatizing banks, allowing private entry, strengthening prudential regulation and supervision, and developing basic financial infrastructure to service a broad segment of the population.

The fiscal space that this opens should be used first to help maintain macroeconomic stability, and then to expand investment in human resources and physical infrastructure, particularly in rural areas (where more than two-thirds of the people in low-income countries live). It would also help finance social safety nets and targeted programs to deal with the transitional costs of privatization and civil service retrenchment.

This strategy departs in important ways from the privatization of small firms and small banks that most low-income countries have adopted—with little impact on macroeconomic aggregates or private investment. The purposes of the new strategy are to restore fiscal stability with minimum job loss, stop the hemorrhaging of the banking system, reduce the crowding out of the private sector, and improve infrastructure services essential for competing in a dynamic global economy. It will also reduce demand on scarce government managerial resources and establish the credibility of the overall reform program.

Many low- and middle-income countries have implemented elements of the complex mosaic of private sector development. And the private sector response has been impressive. But even in countries with well-established institutions and legal systems—and the human resources to translate commitment into action—systemic reform has been a long process (often exceeding 15–20 years) subject to reversal and fragility. Moreover, the poorest countries lack many of the prerequisites—and have little latitude for error. The challenges are particularly daunting in Africa, where the environment for entrepreneurs is highly uncertain, markets are smaller, skills are shallower, the supporting infrastructure is weaker, and the legal and regulatory environment very restricting. The poorest countries thus still need assistance in designing and implementing their reform programs.

Low-income countries are also adapting elements of the reform agenda to their cultural, social, political, economic, and institutional conditions. The report highlights the lessons of experience to contribute to the learning process. But the task of reform is not purely technical. A broad consensus for reform and full government ownership of this difficult long-term agenda are essential for success. And when governments do adopt comprehensive and consistent reforms, donors must be ready to step in, in a coordinated way, with the necessary support to sustain their implementation.

Jean-François Rischard
Vice President
Finance and Private Sector Development
The World Bank

Acknowledgments

THIS report was prepared by a team led by Magdi R. Iskander and comprising Arvind Gupta, Bita Hadjimichael, Kristin Hallberg, John Nellis, Roy Pepper, and Charles Thomas. It drew on background papers prepared by Klaus Deininger, Omer Karasapan, Sunita Kikeri, Clare Narrod, Ousa Sananikone, Dina L. Umali-Deininger, and Douglas Webb. Special thanks for their valuable comments and suggestions go to Mark Baird, A. Basu, Loup Brefort, Gerard Caprio, Paula Donovan, Ahmed Galal, Michael Klein, Johannes Linn, Ignacio Mas, Diana McNaughton, John Page, Gary Perlin, D. C. Rao, Jean-François Rischard, Neil Roger, Enrique Rueda-Sabater, Silvia Sagari, John Shilling, Ernest Stern, Paulo Vieira Da Cunha, Douglas Webb, Michel Wormser, and Roberto Zagha.

The editorial-production team for the report was led by Bruce Ross-Larson and Meta de Coquereaumont, with assistance from Heather Cochran, Julie Harris, Paul Holtz, Heather Imboden, and Debbie Sinmao. Helen Toni was a constant source of assistance and support throughout the project.

Acronyms and abbreviations

AGETIP	Agences d'Exécution des Travaux d'Intérêt Public
CFA	Communauté Financière Africaine
CFAF	Communauté Financière Africaine franc
COE	collectively owned enterprise
CRG	competitiveness review group
DAC	Development Assistance Committee
EMDB	Emerging Markets Data Base
FDI	foreign direct investment
GDP	gross domestic product
GATT	General Agreement on Trade and Tariffs
IBRD	International Bank for Reconstruction and Development
IDA	International Development Association
ICOR	incremental capital-output ratio
IFC	International Finance Corporation
IPA	investment promotion agency
FIAS	Foreign Investment Advisory Service
LTPS	Long-Term Perspective Study
MIGA	Multilateral Investment Guarantee Agency
NGO	nongovernmental organization
OECD	Organization for Economic Cooperation and Development
PSAG	private sector advisory group
QR	quantitative restriction
SME	small and medium-size enterprise
SOE	state-owned enterprise
SPF	State Property Fund
VAT	value-added tax

Definitions and data notes

Definition of low-income countries

For the purpose of this report, all countries eligible for assistance from the International Development Association (IDA) are considered as "low-income." IDA-eligible developing countries are currently defined as those countries with a per capita income of $835 or less in 1993 dollars, although in IDA 10 a small group of island economies in the Caribbean (St. Kitts and Nevis, St. Lucia, and St. Vincent and the Grenadines) and the Pacific (Tonga, Vanuatu, and Western Samoa) with per capita incomes above that level were made eligible for IDA resources to support projects that improve their creditworthiness.

The majority of IDA borrowers fall into the category of "low-income," defined as countries with per capita income of $695 or less. The remainder fall into the category of "lower middle-income," defined as countries with per capita incomes between $696 and $1,345.

Geographic and economic groups

The regional distribution of the 78 IDA-eligible countries is as follows: 41 in Sub-Saharan Africa; 11 in East Asia and the Pacific; 8 in South Asia; 9 in Latin America and the Caribbean; 7 in Eastern Europe and Central Asia; and 2 in Middle East and North Africa. The countries in each region are as follows:

Sub-Saharan Africa. Angola, Benin, Burkina Faso, Burundi, Cape Verde, Cameroon, Central African Republic, Chad, Comoros, Congo, Côte d'Ivoire, Djibouti, Equatorial Guinea, Eritrea, Ethiopia, The Gambia, Ghana, Guinea, Guinea-Bissau, Kenya, Lesotho, Liberia, Madagascar, Malawi, Mali, Mauritania, Mozambique, Niger, Nigeria, Rwanda, São Tomé and

Principe, Senegal, Sierra Leone, Somalia, Sudan, Tanzania, Togo, Uganda, Zaire, Zambia, and Zimbabwe.

The report refers to one subcategory of Sub-Saharan Africa—the CFA franc group, which comprises Benin, Burkina Faso, Cameroon, Central African Republic, Chad, Comoros, Congo, Côte d'Ivoire, Equatorial Guinea, Mali, Niger, Senegal, and Togo.

East Asia and the Pacific. Cambodia, China, Kiribati, Lao People's Democratic Republic, Mongolia, Myanmar, Solomon Islands, Tonga, Vanuatu, Viet Nam, and Western Samoa.

South Asia. Afghanistan, Bangladesh, Bhutan, India, Maldives, Nepal, Pakistan, and Sri Lanka.

Latin America and the Caribbean. Bolivia, Dominica, Grenada, Guyana, Haiti, Honduras, Nicaragua, St. Lucia, and St. Vincent.

Eastern Europe and Central Asia. Albania, Armenia, Azerbaijan, FYR Macedonia, Georgia, Kyrgyz Republic, and Tajikistan.

Middle East and North Africa. Egypt and Yemen.

Analytical groups

For analytical and statistical purposes, the report disaggregates Sub-Saharan Africa into two groups of low-income countries: "reforming economies," which have pursued macroeconomic reform programs, including exchange rate reforms; and "other economies," which have pursued more limited programs. The classification generally follows that used in *Adjustment in Africa: Reforms, Results, and the Road Ahead* (World Bank 1994). The reforming economies are Burundi, The Gambia, Ghana, Guinea, Guinea-Bissau, Kenya, Madagascar, Malawi, Mauritania, Mozambique, Nigeria, Sierra Leone, Tanzania, Uganda, Zambia, and Zimbabwe.

Overview

MANY previously low-income countries have made impressive advances in the past three or four decades. The most successful ones have pursued market-friendly development strategies. Their private sectors have been the engines of growth, generating sustained increases in incomes to allow investments in broadly based and long-term development. And their governments have been focusing on macroeconomic stability, on the business environment, and on basic physical infrastructure and human resources. The results: sustained high growth rates, with widely shared gains in living standards.

Many of today's low-income countries have adopted parts of that strategy, but with major differences in results. Real GDP growth for low-income countries as a group was 5.1 percent a year during 1987–93, and real per capita growth was 3.1 percent—higher than the 3.4 percent and 1.3 percent for other developing countries. Pulling up these averages was the rapid growth in East Asia. South Asian economies were clustered around the average. And economies in Latin America, Sub-Saharan Africa, and Eastern Europe and Central Asia did less well. What stands out are the stagnation of per capita incomes in Sub-Saharan Africa and the steep declines in Eastern Europe and Central Asia.

The variations across countries—in GDP growth, savings, investment, and export growth and diversification—have been enormous (see figures 1–4). The low-income countries doing best have gone beyond broad macroeconomic reforms, conveying to their people—and the world—a commitment to market-oriented economies. They have introduced sustained reform programs to stim-

FIGURE 1 REFORM PRODUCES RESULTS IN LOW-INCOME COUNTRIES

• **China** races ahead to catch middle-income countries within a generation—**other East Asian** countries follow
• **South Asia** picks up, but per capita growth rate is still between one-third and one-half of China's
• **Reforming Africa** recovers, but real per capita growth remains too small to dent poverty—**other African** countries regress

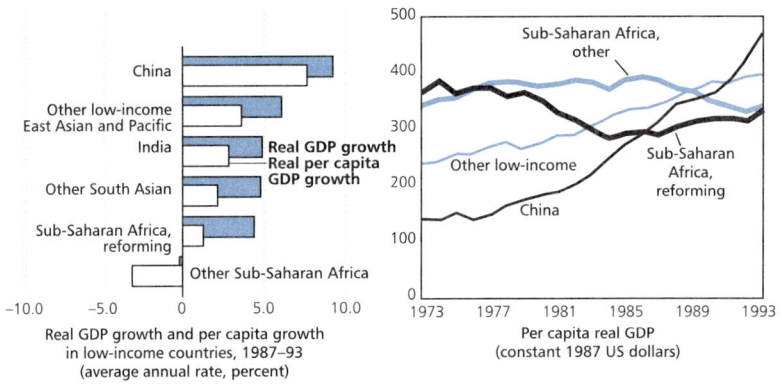

Real GDP growth and per capita growth
in low-income countries, 1987–93
(average annual rate, percent)

Per capita real GDP
(constant 1987 US dollars)

FIGURE 2 DOMESTIC SAVINGS AND FOREIGN DIRECT INVESTMENT FUEL GROWTH

• **China's** spectacular growth is propelled by huge savings and investment, boosted by FDI mainly from overseas Chinese
• **India** and **Pakistan** maintain decent investment, mostly from domestic savings—FDI increases from a low base
• Other **Asian** and **African** countries invest modestly; aid flows are important; FDI is small and mainly in natural resources; domestic savings are limited by wasteful public sector and private sector is wary of harsh business environment

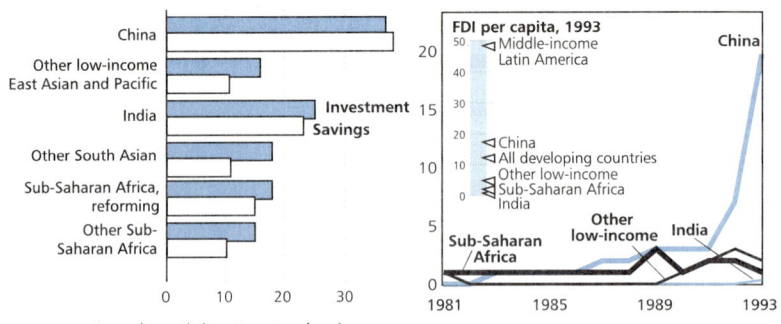

Gross domestic investment and savings
in low-income countries, 1987–93 (percentage of GDP)

Net foreign direct investment (US$ billions)

FIGURE 3 THE PRIVATE SECTOR LEADS THE GROWTH

- **China's** non-state (collectives) and private firms grow at 20 percent a year and account for 75 percent of industrial growth
- **South Asian** industry and services respond nicely to deregulation—agriculture continues steady growth
- In **reforming Africa** agriculture grows at rates comparable to China's and South Asia's—private sector picks up in industry and services
- **Other Africa** stagnates

Average annual percentage growth, 1987–93

ulate internal and external competition and private investment by locals and foreigners. And they have succeeded in creating vibrant private sectors in a relatively short time.

The best performers have been in Asia. China's growth has been particularly spectacular, with real GDP growing at 9.3 percent a year and real per capita income at 7.8 percent during 1987–93. Building on past investments in human, physical, and institutional capital, that growth was the result of an ambitious, comprehensive, and sustained program. Reforms liberalized agriculture, redirected a large part of savings to the provinces, removed price controls, made economic zones attractive manufacturing platforms for export, and gradually liberalized trade and started to revamp the tax and financial systems.

In South Asia, major economies grew by about 5 percent a year, permitting real per capita incomes to increase by about 3 percent a year. Fueling the growth were savings and investment rates of around 20 percent, mainly from domestic sources building on strong legal and political traditions and a growing pool of technical skills. Deregulation and trade reform increased internal competition, reduced production costs, and improved product range and quality.

The increased private activity in Asia has stimulated the financial sector and is beginning to attract substantial foreign investment, particularly in infrastructure and the stock market.

FIGURE 4 OUTWARD ORIENTATION STIMULATES GROWTH, HELPS DIVERSIFY ECONOMIES

• **China's** exports surge at 30 percent a year—firms with FDI account for 36 percent of exports, helping China become world's tenth–largest trading nation
• **India's** manufacturing exports pick up to slightly larger share of world exports—**Pakistan** and **Sri Lanka** follow
• **Other countries,** dependent on a few commodities, stagnate and lose market share to more competitive producers in Asia and Latin America; with little diversification they become more susceptible to terms of trade shocks

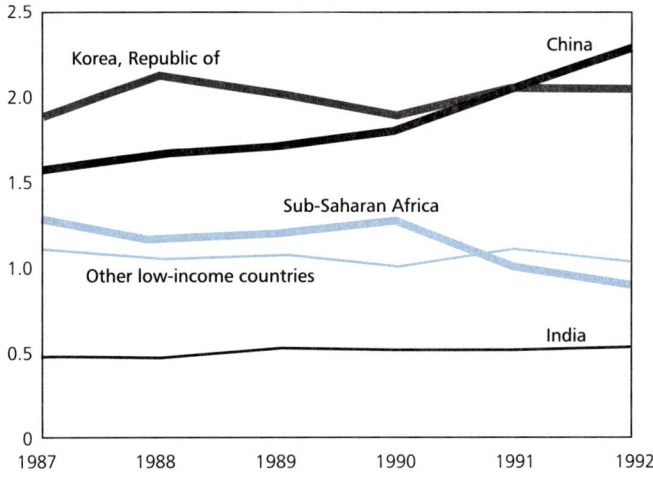

Merchandise exports (percentage of world exports)

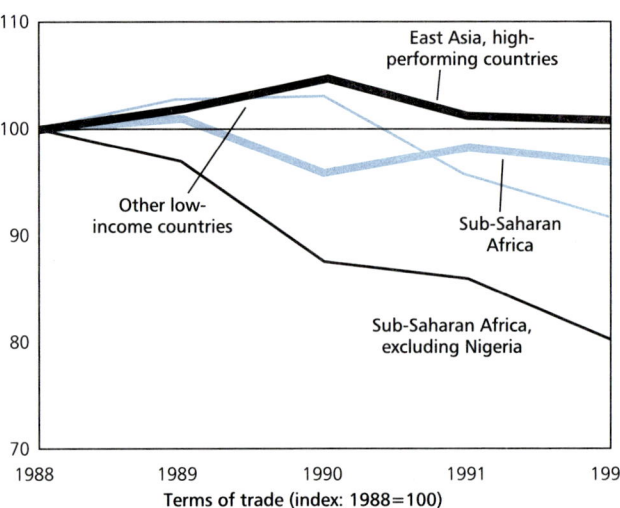

Terms of trade (index: 1988=100)

In Sub-Saharan Africa, real GDP grew at 2.2 percent a year during 1987–93, but real per capita income fell by 0.9 percent a year because of rapid population growth. This regional average masks considerable diversity. Of the reforming economies, the best performers had GDP growth rates close to those in South Asia. But with population growth of about 3.0 percent a year, per capita GDP in reforming economies increased by only 1.3 percent a year between 1987 and 1993. The other African countries had GDP declines of 0.2 percent a year and per capita declines of 3.2 percent a year—as agriculture, industry, and services stagnated. They include countries torn by civil war and social unrest as well as potentially rich countries that have suffered from fiscal excesses, overvalued exchange rates, poor governance, and capital flight.

Reforming African countries made considerable strides in reversing policies that had previously stifled private initiative

Reforming African countries made considerable strides in reversing policies that had previously led to rapid declines in living standards, undermined institutions fundamental to the proper functioning of markets, and stifled private initiative. Supported by substantial external aid, they liberalized exchange rates, removed import restrictions, and gradually reduced tariffs—gradually because of their importance for fiscal revenue and a perceived need to phase in reductions in effective protection. They also removed price controls on agricultural products, and most manufactured product prices were decontrolled, except for petroleum—where government involvement has been extremely costly, especially in countries with refineries. In the financial sectors, steps were taken to reduce financial repression, improve supervisory and regulatory frameworks, and address financial distress in the banks.

The primary source of growth in reforming Africa was the private sector. Agricultural growth was close to that in China and South Asia. Small enterprises in industry and services, particularly the informal sector, gained because of increased access to production inputs, raising the demand for labor and increasing the low-wage employment in the informal sector. But the supply response in the formal economy, particularly in private savings and investment, has been muted by basic deficiencies in infrastructure and human resources and lack of confidence in the permanence of reform. The reason: few governments have undertaken the necessary structural reforms, particularly to improve a harsh business environment, reduce the dominance and losses of the public enterprises, develop a robust and competitive financial system, and upgrade infrastructure services.

In Africa as a whole, the fiscal drain of public enterprises and the losses of the financial system can be as high as 8–12 percent of GDP—2–3 times the spending on health and education and about two-thirds of gross investment. So, few resources remain for private or public investment to upgrade the weak base of human resources and infrastructure. And that has severely limited the ability of a weak and fragmented private sector to respond to macroeconomic reforms (even with a considerable depreciation of real exchange rates). Even in reforming Africa, public sector inefficiencies have reduced GDP growth by at least 2–3 percentage points, limited the opportunities for job growth, and exacerbated the social costs of adjustment. This in turn has weakened popular support for difficult economic reforms and the governments' resolve to sustain them.

These public sector losses—plus major expenditures on large and inefficient civil services—were primarily responsible for the fiscal instabilities that have contributed to the stop-and-go reforms characterizing many African economies. The resulting uncertainty was further compounded by excessive reliance on foreign aid—which, though crucial to support macroeconomic reforms and long-term investment needs, put a damper on domestic and foreign investors' confidence in the permanence of reform. So, in most African countries foreign direct investment (FDI) was confined to enclave operations in mining and petroleum.

By contrast, the better performers in Asia started with more developed industrial and service sectors. They also had better infrastructure and more skilled human resources. And they often had larger markets and stronger institutions. The private sector in these economies, particularly in industry and services, responded strongly to gradual and often partial policy changes.

The Asian countries also enjoyed high domestic savings and investments and relied only moderately on foreign aid. Macroeconomic imbalances did occur as a result of fiscal slippages and the fiscal deficits of public enterprises. But the economic impact was smaller—public enterprises' fiscal deficits were 5 percent of GDP in India and 3–5 percent in China during 1987–93, compared with gross domestic investment of 25 percent and 39 percent, respectively. And the solutions to difficult and pressing problems were more under their control. Their track records raised the confidence of domestic and foreign investors allowing the countries to achieve macroeconomic balance through their own efforts.

China's spectacular growth reflects high domestic savings and investment rates—12–15 percentage points above India's, and bringing an additional 3–4 percentage points in GDP growth. It also reflects a major outward reorientation, with merchandise exports growing at 30 percent annually and a large influx of FDI, mainly from overseas Chinese. Totaling about $50 billion over the past ten years, FDI contributed about 60 percent of gross capital formation in the coastal zones. In 1993, firms with FDI accounted for $36 billion of China's $100 billion in exports.

The imperatives of faster growth, led by the private sector

Given the severity of poverty and the pace of population growth, most low-income countries have no choice but to accelerate economic growth, if they are to provide new job opportunities and reduce unemployment. The respectable GDP growth rates of successful performers in Sub-Saharan Africa are not enough to make a serious dent in poverty—or to generate enough new, productive jobs to replace those that may be lost initially through privatization or civil service reform. With population increases of 3 percent a year, GDP growth of 4–5 percent means per capita increases of only 1–2 percent. At this rate, it will take low-income countries more than half a century to reach the living standards of today's middle-income countries.

The keys to accelerated growth are much higher investments and domestic savings, combined with systemic structural reforms to improve productivity

In addition to slower population growth, GDP growth of 7–8 percent in real terms—with the benefits shared widely—is needed to reduce significantly the number of people living in absolute poverty below the current level of one billion. Rapid growth is also needed to maintain harmony among different groups competing for their share of the economic pie in increasingly pluralistic political systems.

The reform agenda

The keys to accelerated growth are much higher investments and domestic savings, combined with systematic structural reforms—necessary to maintain macroeconomic stability and significantly improve productivity. The slow-growing economies need to raise their savings and investment rates from the current 12–16 percent of GDP to at least 20–25 percent—levels already achieved or exceeded by India, Kenya, and Zimbabwe. Initially most of the change will have to come from reducing government dissaving—since the private sector usually responds slowly to sustained reform.

Major changes will thus have to be made in the size and structure of government revenues and expenditures. Raising revenues calls for measures to broaden the tax base—by simplifying tax regimes, abolishing exemptions, reducing the discretionary authority of tax and customs administrators, and improving collection capacity. But the biggest impact will come from reducing the budget outlays on public enterprises and stopping the leakages from the banking system—which eat up most domestic savings in many African countries.

The strategy for moving low-income economies from state dominance to competitive markets—broadly outlined in figures 5 and 6—includes:

- *Going farther and faster on public sector reform* by accelerating the privatization, closure, or liquidation of the 10–15 largest enterprises that account for most of the fiscal losses, environmental degradation, and the leakages from the banking system, while employing only a small fraction of the labor force. These enterprises typically are the utilities (telecommunications and power), petroleum refiners and distributors, heavy industrial manufacturers, and agricultural marketing boards.

- *Focusing the public expenditure program* on public goods and cutting out investments that the private sector could better undertake.

- *Accelerating financial sector reform* by severing the links between banks and nonperforming borrowers—whether public or private. The key steps in this are to privatize banks, allow new entry, strengthen prudential regulation and supervision, and develop basic financial infrastructure.

These measures will help—with minimum job loss—to restore fiscal stability, stop the hemorrhaging of the banking system, and reduce the crowding out of the private sector. They will also improve infrastructure services essential to a competitive private sector, reduce the demand on scarce government managerial resources, and establish the credibility of reforms.

The resulting fiscal space should be used, first, to maintain macrostability to avoid the stop-and-go policies that so often undermine the confidence of the private sector—and to expand long-term investment in people and infrastructure, particularly in rural areas, where most people live. It will also help provide social safety nets.

In parallel with these efforts, private sector development requires a more favorable, yet competitive, business environment. An array of policy, legal, regulatory, and institutional reforms are needed to stimulate competition and dismantle onerous regulations that increase transaction costs by as much as 30 percent, and often more. Such increased competition—essential for promoting agile firms that can adapt to changes in global markets—is the driving force for productivity growth.

Many elements of this agenda—which shifts the emphasis from preserving jobs in an inefficient public sector to creating jobs in a vibrant private sector—have been implemented in many low- and middle-income countries. And the response of the private sector has been impressive.

Economies that have already accelerated their growth rates and made a start on institutional and structural reforms have some leeway—to take a more gradual approach to solving their remaining problems. But the least developed and

FIGURE 5 IMPLEMENTING THE PRIVATE SECTOR DEVELOPMENT AGENDA . . .

FROM DOMINANT STATE...

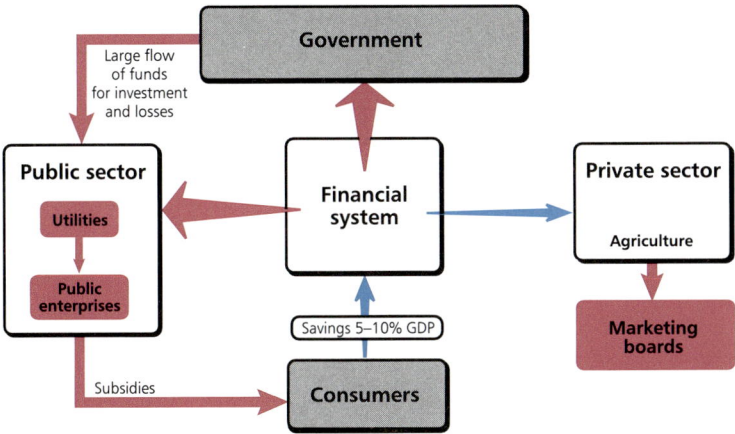

Overbearing public sector

- Utilities and large public enterprises absorb a large share of government resources
- They crowd out investment in social sectors and infrastructure, particularly in rural areas
- Public enterprise and large urban consumers receive bulk of subsidies provided by utilities

Distressed financial system

- Fiscal deficits, public enterprises, and privileged private firms drain system
- Remaining private sector crowded out
- Public sector banks dominate, with large amounts of nonperforming loans
- Financial repression provides little incentive for savings
- Weak prudential regulation and supervision

Harsh business environment

- Weak legal system
- Private sector overregulated and overprotected
- Incentives and regulations unevenly applied
- Agriculture oppressed by price controls and marketing boards
- Goods and services provided by public sector increase the cost of private firms by 20–30 percent

FIGURE 6 . . . A LONG AND WINDING ROAD

...TO COMPETITIVE MARKETS

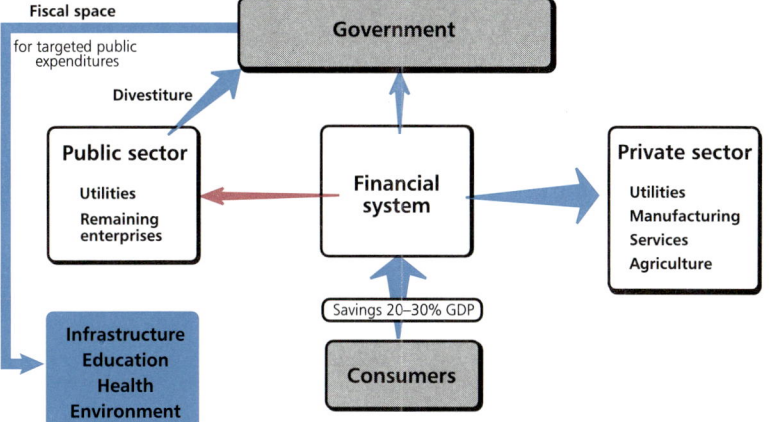

Reformed public sector

- Rationalize subsidies; target them to poor
- Sell large public enterprises on a priority basis; use sales proceeds to retire debt
- Attract private sector in utilities (requires pricing reform, competition, and regulation)
- Operate remaining public enterprises on commercial basis
- Prune public expenditures and focus them on public goods

Robust financial system

- Cut off nonperforming borrowers—public and private—from further credit; make a vigorous collection effort
- Privatize banks and allow new entry by reputable banks
- Build payment systems
- Strengthen prudential regulation and supervision
- Serve small savers and borrowers

Attractive business environment

- Reform legal and regulatory system
- Reform tax and customs administration
- Deregulate economy to complement liberalization of internal and external trade
- Promote foreign investment and regional integration
- Conduct these activities in partnership with the private sector and labor

the slowest growers have no such luxury. The fragility of their economies means that if some crucial element is missing, progress is likely to be limited and easily reversed. Their private sector development agenda is thus very broad, requiring simultaneous and often unpopular actions in many areas over long periods. Successful reform and development will rest largely on these countries' own efforts. But external assistance remains vital to help reforming economies preserve macroeconomic and political stability—and to invest in long-term growth.

Though pivotal, private sector development is only one part of sustainable development, which encompasses such other areas as health, education, infrastructure, and environmental protection. These topics are treated in other periodic and special reports.

This report presents the rationale for the strategy proposed (the why), its main elements (the what), and experience in implementing them (the how). It contributes to the learning process by showing how countries have adapted the menu of solutions to their cultural, social, political, economic, and institutional conditions.

Privatizing and commercializing public enterprises

Almost all low-income countries need urgently to reduce the budgetary drain of public enterprises and to put their physical—and human—resources to more efficient use. Their past efforts at reform, short of privatization, rarely produced the desired results. So, many of them turned to privatization, but almost none has divested an economically significant portion of its public enterprise sector. Yet, in the few instances where large private investors have been attracted (in power in Pakistan, for example), there has been significant impact on macroeconomic aggregates.

Simultaneous action is needed on both fronts—public enterprise reform and privatization are not "either-or" propositions

Needed now are stronger actions to reform public enterprises and faster and deeper programs of privatization—to produce macroeconomic improvement through major reductions in fiscal deficits and general improvements in business conditions. Simultaneous action is needed on both fronts—public enterprise reform and privatization are not "either-or" propositions.

Countries succeeding in this process have avoided investments in the public sector that could better be handled by the private sector—and imposed a hard budget constraint on the remaining public enterprises. Experience reveals that the way forward is to:

■   Sell public enterprises producing tradables and operating in competitive markets. (If they cannot be sold, they should be liquidated.) Prime candidates are the largest public enterprises having adverse impacts on the budget and the economy—the banks, the large manufacturing enterprises, the marketing boards, and the procurement, refining, and distribution of petroleum products. Even where proceeds might be modest, as in much of Africa, ending the financial drain is the important point.

■   Involve the private sector in the commercialization, management, financing, and as much as possible in the ownership of infrastructure— as in China, India, and Pakistan.

Focus on the larger enterprises

Why the focus on the largest public firms? Because privatizing them immediately reduces the fiscal deficit, improves public saving, and demonstrates the government's commitment to reform.

Infrastructure utilities are particularly attractive candidates for divestiture

---

Divestiture is neither a panacea nor an end in itself. But done well, it is a powerful tool that not only brings better performance at the level of the firm, it also helps repatriate flight capital, attract foreign direct investment, and broaden and deepen access to international capital markets. These positive macroeconomic effects are enhanced when privatization's proceeds are devoted to reducing the high-cost government debt that is crowding out the private sector and increasing real interest rates.

Infrastructure utilities are particularly attractive candidates for divestiture. The financial, economic, and psychological impact of increased private involvement is generally large. The need for improved services is incontestable—consumers always applaud increases in the quality or reliability of services. And investors are willing and able to act. Moreover, privatizing infrastructure services facing growing demand—such as telecommunications or power—typically results in little loss of employment. And efficiency still rises because of increased investment and proper pricing.

Particularly in Sub-Saharan Africa, however, the situation is much more difficult. Product markets are less competitive. Capital markets are thin. Investors perceive high risks. And public enterprises in infrastructure have a lower net worth and are less attractive to foreign buyers, except perhaps in telecommunications. Governments resist selling to foreigners, and investors are reluctant to take an equity position in infrastructure firms before governments have established consistent policy and pricing practices. These serious obstacles delay or dilute reform. What can be done to overcome them?

Addressing the causes of delay—lessons of experience

To speed the reform process, successful governments have taken the following actions:

- First, they have persisted with and deepened macroeconomic reforms—establishing new relative prices, enhancing competitive forces, and creating opportunities for job and income generation. This hastens the sale of small and medium-size firms. To obtain private involvement in larger firms, reforming governments have put trade and regulatory frameworks in order, thus attracting new entrants, stimulating competition in markets, and mitigating monopoly abuse in non-competitive markets.

- Second, they have made efforts to inform their citizens—especially such opinion-leaders and decisionmakers as legislators, journalists, and university professors—of the high costs of inaction in public enterprise reform. And they have undertaken public relations campaigns and sponsored study trips to reforming countries to build public support for change and reveal the potential of reform and divestiture. These efforts have often mobilized popular support and broken the opposition of vested interests.

- Third, they have used methods of sale combining core investors with such broad ownership vehicles as trust funds, share giveaways, employee ownership options, and other devices—to enlist widespread participation in and approval for the privatization process. These methods address fears that only foreigners, the elite, or members of particular ethnic groups benefit from privatization.

- Fourth, they have streamlined—indeed privatized—the privatization process, by keeping the public sales agency lean and agile and by contracting out the details of implementation to private lawyers, accountants, and investment bankers both local and foreign. (Policy decisions remain firmly in government hands.) This approach gains time, produces quality work, gives assurance to investors—and develops local capabilities and the consulting business. Having worked in settings as varied as Mexico, Morocco, and Russia, it is now being tried in Ghana.

- Fifth, where privatization has proven difficult or not yet possible, particularly for infrastructure firms, they have made greater use of methods of privatizing management—such as asset leasing, franchising, concessions, and management contracts. (Governments obtain the economic benefits of private control without paying the political costs of losing ownership.) Where the value of physical assets is low, the franchise value of infrastructure networks may still be substantial. Divestiture's net positive impact on the economy can still be considerable.

Bringing the legal and institutional frameworks to a higher level of working order is a fundamental but complex task

- Sixth, recognizing the importance and difficulty of putting good regulatory systems in place, they have adapted regulatory structures to fit market conditions and institutional capabilities (and they have seen that it is usually more difficult for a government to directly manage a public enterprise than to regulate and monitor it).
- Seventh, they have begun to unbundle ancillary or social assets from enterprises and to transfer them to the private sector or to the responsible level of government. This is particularly relevant in transition economies, where public enterprises traditionally provided many social services—housing, education, health facilities.
- Eighth, they have established severance funds, training programs, and other elements of a social safety net—to assist those laid off in the reform process.
- Ninth, with donors and the international financial community, they are trying, selectively, to give limited comfort to investors through guarantees (particularly for the policy risks in large infrastructure operations) and insurance schemes.

These are the steps that low-income countries should be taking, and in many cases are.

Addressing the less technical obstacles

As this reform process unfolds, it is clear that the role of government remains crucial. To succeed, privatization requires transparency in transactions, good competition policies and regulatory frameworks, and careful management of social and political consequences. All these are functions of the political system. In all low-income countries, bringing the legal and institutional frameworks to a higher level of working order is a fundamental but complex task that calls for redoubling the efforts of reforming governments and the donors.

A fundamental obstacle to divestiture and public enterprise reform in low-income countries has been concern that the "winners" in the process would be the few, the foreign, or the elite—while the "losers" would be the many, the indigenous, and the workers. Studies of privatizations in middle-income countries show these fears to be exaggerated. Gains outweigh losses, winners outnumber losers, workers and locals do as well as foreign investors. It may not be possible to obtain the same results in the more constrained settings of low-income countries. But that does not mean that the socio-political obstacles to reform are insurmountable.

There is much that governments—and donors—can do to accelerate and deepen the reform and privatization process. A good place to start is to shed light on the performance and costs of public enterprises—with their implicit subsidies, their concessional lending rates, the losses they inflict on the banking system, and the frequent need for government to assume their debts and arrears. In too many instances, this information has not been systematically collected and analyzed. Doing so would publicly expose the cost of inaction and provide governments with the ammunition needed to launch reform programs.

Building robust financial systems

Many low-income countries made substantial efforts in the 1980s to reverse policies that undermined their financial systems. They reduced fiscal deficits, strengthened central banks' conduct of monetary and financial sector policies, gradually freed interest rates, eliminated credit ceilings, reduced directed credit, and restructured banks—albeit at high cost.

But these measures produced limited results, and the financial systems in most low-income economies remain very weak. Rudimentary payment and settlement systems hinder commerce, as does a severe lack of banking skills—especially for credit appraisal. Most financial systems are still dominated by state-owned banks, subject to little competition and supervision. Typically, more than 50 percent of domestic credit goes to the public sector. And credit to the private sector is garnered by large and politically well-connected firms and traders. Farmers and small firms are left to finance growth from retained earnings.

The agenda: address the fundamentals

Building effective financial systems in low-income countries will take a long time—given the lack of skills, poor institutional and regulatory capacity, and the pernicious links between financial and public enterprises. Needed first is a solid foundation of banking infrastructure—sound and effective payment systems and accounting, auditing, and supervisory systems. The biggest challenge, however, is to restructure the banking system in a way that minimizes the cost to the taxpayer, reduces the likelihood of recurring crises, and develops sound and competitive banking and nonbanking systems that provide basic services to the whole population. These services include, on a priority basis, safe and secure savings (particularly in rural areas), reliable payment systems, and working capital finance, especially trade finance.

Sever the link between banks and loss-makers

The first and most difficult task in restructuring the banking system is to sever the link between state banks, which still dominate the banking system, and nonperforming borrowers—by cutting them off from new credit and collecting outstanding loans. In practice, it has proved difficult, if not impossible, for state banks to enforce a hard budget constraint on large enterprises and cooperatives. Central bank attempts to enforce credit ceilings often result in large inter-enterprise arrears. When these arrears accumulate and threaten the solvency of banks and enterprises, the central bank is forced to relax credit. The result is that state banks continue to accumulate large losses and have to be recapitalized frequently.

The first and most difficult task in restructuring the banking system is to sever the link between state banks and nonperforming borrowers

The drain of big loss-making enterprises is likely to worsen as they face increased competition from imports and domestic private producers. That underscores the urgency of privatizing these enterprises and using the proceeds to reduce the high-cost government debt that crowds out the private sector and increases real lending rates. The proceeds could also be used to restore the integrity of the contractual savings system that governments have often raided to finance their deficits.

Go beyond recapitalization

One of the main reasons that restructuring the banking system often fails is that governments normally bear the entire cost—stopping short of changing the incentive system and the structure of the banking sector. Losses are seldom shared with other stakeholders. Nor are loan recovery efforts vigorous. In most cases, restructuring merely transfers nonperforming loans to recovery agencies, where they languish uncollected.

By contrast, successful restructuring has been accompanied by changes in the incentive system. This involves bank privatization and changes in management, since it is much easier to establish an arm's length relationship between properly regulated and supervised private banks and their clients.

Reduce the role of state banks and stimulate competition

In general, privatization and liquidation have proved easier for small and medium-size banks, particularly when part of an overall reform program that allows new entry. Pakistan and some African countries in the CFA zone are cases in point.

But in small countries particularly, liquidating or privatizing state banks that account for the bulk of banking system assets is difficult—both economically and politically. What can be done? Maintaining the dominant position of big banks, even while allowing new entry, does little to change their performance. An alternative is to downsize them and to seek management contracts from reputable domestic and foreign banks, preferably with a preferred equity position, to run them until improvements attract suitable buyers. Some governments are considering breaking larger state banks into competing networks—as they were before their nationalization in the 1960s and 1970s—that service both urban and rural areas and sell them to reputable buyers.

Attracting reputable private banks will be difficult, however, unless government reduces the dominant position of public enterprises and develops an attractive environment to stimulate the private sector. Indeed, a good part of the banking development in China, India, Pakistan, and Sri Lanka has been stimulated by the growth of a competitive private sector that demands a wider range of efficiently delivered services. In turn, a competitive banking system helps foster a competitive private sector, since borrowers are not limited to a few banks that service only selected and well-connected clients. And the presence of foreign banks has helped promote and facilitate FDI.

Still, bank privatization, if not done well, carries risks. In some cases, banks have been sold to privileged buyers less than transparently in an unregulated environment. In other cases, banks have been sold with little information about the quality of the portfolio. This underscores what is needed for privatization to succeed. Banks should be sold in a transparent manner only to qualified and reputable buyers who have access to the necessary information. They then have to be properly regulated and supervised. And they should not be bailed out if they fail. In many low-income countries, the difficulty of restructuring and privatizing banks is often compounded by ethnic considerations, and privatization methods should include ways to broaden ownership.

Strengthen prudential regulation and supervision

Most low-income countries have strengthened their banking laws and regulations, and some have improved their supervisory and enforcement powers. But the information and skills needed to apply these standards remain limited and will take time to develop. As an interim step, some countries—such as Bolivia and India—have successfully used twinning or subcontracting arrangements with central banks and accounting firms to supplement and speed up the building of their own capabilities.

Creating an inviting environment for business

In a world where technological change is reducing transport costs, hastening globalization, and changing the nature of competition, firms must be agile and acquire new skills to survive and grow. Yet firm-level surveys for private sector assessments document the maze of restrictive regulations—covering labor, pricing, licensing, investment, monopoly privileges, fiscal and tax incentives, and so on—that continue to segment markets and encourage rent seeking, illegality, and corruption. The consistent message from these surveys: the cost of doing business is high, particularly for small and new enterprises.

In many low-income countries, the central challenge for government is to cut risks and transaction costs and to instill confidence in the private sector—confidence that the business environment will change. A first step is to signal an unequivocal commitment to this goal at the highest political level. As a practical expression of the commitment, government can consult business leaders and groups (through public-private discussion councils) to identify major reform needs. While the precise reform agenda varies widely—reflecting the progress of policy reform and the extent of regulatory and institutional interventions in business activities—there are four common key areas for improving the business environment:
- Strengthening the legal and judicial system.
- Reducing the barriers to competition and improving regulation.
- Supporting entrepreneurial development.
- Promoting global integration through foreign direct investment and regional integration to complement trade reform.

Strengthen the legal and judicial system

For some low-income transitional economies, such as Albania, China, and Viet Nam, the legal underpinnings of a market economy must be built. But for most, the task is to remedy deficiencies in the existing framework.

The main deficiencies relate to legislative, judicial, and administrative processes necessary to ensure that laws support the public interest and private economic rights and are enforced equitably and expeditiously. In many countries, the enactment and enforcement of laws for arbitration, intellectual property, debt recovery, and collateral are typically inhibited by the lack of appropriate legal institutions, procedures, and qualified personnel. Even routine and minor commercial disputes take years to settle, because procedures for rendering and enforcing judgments are protracted and alternative dispute resolution mechanisms are ineffective. Enforcement is also constrained by poorly trained staff and run-down facilities. Effective enforcement of laws will require revision of civil and penal procedure codes, reorganization of administrative systems, and greater investment in physical and human capital.

Reduce barriers to competition and deregulate product and factor markets

Competition, a driving force for creating agile firms, is fundamental for efficient private sector development. If firms are to court markets for profit and not the state for favors, deregulation is essential for promoting competitive markets. And wherever trade liberalization has been accompanied by measures to reduce the administrative impediments to exports and the cost of doing business, the supply response has been considerable.

Liberalize external and internal trade. Many low-income countries have made notable progress in liberalizing external trade by reducing trade and non-tariff barriers for both imports and exports. In particular, African countries have removed almost all quantitative restrictions. But most countries have adopted a gradual approach to reducing tariffs. Many low-income countries, again particularly in Africa, have also liberalized the rules governing internal commerce, removing most price controls and restrictive policies limiting private entry and marketing.

The major impact of liberalizing trade has been to give firms easier access to capital, technology, intermediate goods, and critical raw materials. This has increased internal competition, reduced production costs, improved product range and quality, and boosted exports.

One concern often expressed by governments and the private sector is that rapid liberalization will lead to deindustrialization, decimate small and medium-size industries, and retard the growth of budding domestic entrepreneurs. Indeed, some firms do suffer when incentives change—especially inefficient, capital-intensive public enterprises that have developed behind tariff barriers and that might see their domestic market shrink as a result of import competition. But in many countries, exemptions and quantitative restrictions abound, particularly in Asia. And tariffs remain high—it is not unusual to find effective rates of protection between 40–60 percent. This inhibits exports and mutes competition in domestic markets.

Much of this protection is eroded by the high cost of doing business stemming from onerous regulatory requirements, high financing costs, and the poor quality and high cost of supply from the public sector. The solution is not to have more selective protection, which requires a competent civil service to implement, monitor, and adapt effectively. Instead, the emphasis has to be on systematically reducing the costs of excessive economic and administrative regulations. This would complement continuing efforts to lower the effective rates of protection, reduce the dispersion in tariffs, eliminate quantitative restrictions, and remove impediments to internal trade. Among these impediments are government monopolies and the privileged access of public enterprises and well-connected firms to finance and to markets.

The emphasis has to be on systematically reducing the costs of excessive economic and administrative regulations

---

Reform regulation and deregulate. Many countries have started the long process of regulatory reform—generally by simplifying taxes, eliminating licensing for investment, and improving the tax and customs administration. Experiences in most cases have been positive—with increased tax revenues and generally higher private investment. Reforms in these regulations frequently need to be complemented by reform in labor markets to allow firms more flexibility in restructuring their operations and responding to changing competition. To increase investor confidence, deregulation should be done through systematic search and dismantle campaigns—in joint efforts with the private sector.

Support entrepreneurship

There is no shortage of entrepreneurs in low-income countries. Most of them are found in agriculture, industry, and services—and mainly in small firms in the informal sector, where many are women. And although small entrepreneurs have benefited from liberalization and deregulation, they still need special support to grow—not protection, which has failed in so many countries, but easy access to markets, finance, and technical know-how.

Most small firms acquire their capabilities in the normal course of operating their businesses. A large part of their know-how comes from suppliers, traders, and larger companies. Beyond that, experience shows that well-focused technical assistance from productivity centers and extension services can make a difference. Some countries are thus redirecting their technological infrastructure from expensive basic and applied research to activities that help improve the productivity of their industries. Many countries could benefit from a similar shift.

Small entrepreneurs still need easy access
to markets, finance, and technical know-how

There are also an increasing number of specialized financial institutions—credit unions, nongovernmental organizations (NGOs), and so on—that rely on local savings, reliable banking services, careful screening of borrowers, and lending at market rates to reach a large number of small clients, particularly women. Gradually replacing costly subsidized credit programs, which have often failed to reach the intended targets, these budding institutions need temporary help (seed or equity capital and technical assistance for small entrepreneurs) to grow, to evolve into licensed financial institutions, and to have refinancing facilities with banks. The better ones with long track records are starting to tap capital markets and attract private investors.

Promote foreign direct investment

Foreign direct investment can be critical in introducing widespread technological change, improving the agility and competitiveness of firms, and providing access to skills and global markets. This is evident in China, and to a lesser extent in Bangladesh, India, and Kenya, where FDI is increasingly generating spillover effects in many sectors. Successful cases show the importance of having governments promote and welcome FDI, particularly in infrastructure such as communications and energy. They also show the importance of avoiding excessive regulation and restrictions on expatriates and financial flows and the business activities of firms.

The need for FDI is greatest in Sub-Saharan Africa, but little has been received outside the enclaves of mining and oil. Indeed, there is concern about considerable foreign disinvestment from Africa in response to the uncertain political and economic environment, the high cost of doing business, and the fears that policies and regulations discriminate against foreign investors, who have many other opportunities all over the world. FDI inflows and FDI stock already in the country would benefit from a more stable and dynamic environment—and a willingness to accept investment from all sources, including minorities and ethnic groups.

Promote regional integration

There are strong aspirations for regional integration in Africa. Indeed, many countries are starting to coordinate and harmonize policies for tariffs, taxation, investment, and business regulations. But the biggest and most productive impetus to regional integration would come from removing the restrictions on movements of goods, capital, and people. These restrictions have severely limited trade and encouraged smuggling. In addition, there is considerable untapped potential for regional cooperation in power, transport, and the distribution of petroleum products (oil and gas) to reduce the costs of supplying these services.

Regional integration is also likely to get a boost from the development of regional growth poles—South Africa and Zimbabwe in the south, Côte d'Ivoire, Ghana, and Nigeria in the west, and Kenya, Tanzania, and Uganda in the east. These could produce important pull effects on growth throughout the continent if the limitations and impediments on local and foreign investors and movements of goods, people, and capital are removed. They would also help promote FDI by enlarging markets. But regional integration should not be a substitute for opening up to the global economy. It should be seen as the way to help firms connect to global markets at lower cost.

Supporting implementation

The strategy outlined here implies a major change in the role of the government—from an owner and operator to a policymaker and regulator that works closely with the private sector in developing a competitive, outward-looking economy. Fundamental to the success of this orientation is accelerating the efforts of many governments to build competent and agile institutions that can help firms respond quickly to changing market conditions.

This accelerated growth strategy stresses going farther and faster on the privatization of enterprises and banks and on economic deregulation. It redirects scarce managerial and institutional resources within government so that it can concentrate on providing basic public goods that only government can provide and that have been neglected in the past. Beyond the government institutions responsible for macroeconomic management, the most important are those for enacting and enforcing legal and regulatory systems, for providing public finance in close interaction with the private sector, for dealing with trade and investment, and for supporting technological development, particularly for small and medium-size firms. In fast-growing countries, these institutions have worked closely and regularly with business and labor associations and other civic groups to solve problems that affect the ability of firms to compete effectively both internally and externally.

Even in countries that have well-established legal, institutional, and human resources to underpin a strong political commitment, systemic reform has been fraught with difficulties. It is a fragile, long-term process—often taking 15–20 years—subject to many reversals. The poorest countries, however, lack these resources, and thus have little latitude for error. Entrepreneurs in Africa are particularly disadvantaged. Their environment is highly uncertain, markets are smaller, skills are shallower, the supporting infrastructure is weaker, and the legal and regulatory environment very restricting. Not only must the poorest countries lay strong foundations for private sector growth through intensive efforts to develop their human capital and physical infrastructure, but they must also persist in this effort over a long period to achieve sustained, visible results.

Over this long haul, government ownership of the reform program and a broad consensus for reform are the products of public-private partnerships and the prerequisites for success. But low-income countries will still need assistance to design, implement, and sustain reform programs. Wherever governments do adopt comprehensive and consistent reform plans, donors must be ready to step in, in a coordinated way, with all necessary support for the sustained implementation of reforms. Where these plans are still being formulated, donors should focus their support on helping governments lay the foundation for change.

CHAPTER 1

From state to market—uneven progress

THE development strategies of most low-income countries in the 1960s and 1970s emphasized import-substituting industrialization with economic growth led by the state. Public enterprises dominated strategic industries, and publicly owned banks served as conduits of financial flows to prop up the enterprises. Governments generated resources by taxing agriculture and trade.

This model of development had early successes, but it was increasingly viewed as ineffective in the late 1970s and early 1980s, as economic growth slowed. Many low-income countries found themselves with large fiscal deficits and overvalued exchange rates that were unsustainable.

Recent policy reforms

Reforming low-income countries responded by implementing reform programs that emphasized macroeconomic stability, openness to trade, and price deregulation. Exchange rate reforms have eliminated large black market premiums in countries where the official exchange rate had been kept artificially low. Nominal devaluations, leading to large real exchange rate depreciations, and reduced rationing of foreign exchange, often through auctions, have been among the biggest changes. The devaluation of the CFA franc in January 1994 symbolized the changing consensus on exchange rate policy in Africa.

Trade reform has been a central part of these reform packages. To liberalize imports, governments largely started by removing foreign exchange rationing and nontariff barriers such as licensing and quotas. For tariff barriers, most governments have adopted a gradual approach—both because of the importance of trade taxes for revenues and because firms need to adjust to reductions in effective protection. Progress often has focused on simplifying tariff codes and reducing maximum rates. On the export side, there has been movement on reducing export taxes—and several governments raised farmgate prices even as world prices for export crops fell.

Trade reforms have been complemented by domestic pricing reforms in Africa, generally reducing the number of goods subject to price control. Most price controls on agricultural outputs have been lifted, although only half the reforming economies have removed price controls and subsidies for fertilizer. The marketing of staples (except maize) has been liberalized in almost all countries. Most manufactured products have been decontrolled, except for petroleum, where government involvement is extremely costly, especially in countries with refineries.

Reforming low-income countries responded by implementing reform programs that emphasized macroeconomic stability, openness to trade, and price deregulation

---

Most reforming countries in Africa have also improved their monetary policies. But delays in dealing with fiscal deficits, which came from weak tax revenues and public sector losses, have put a disproportionate burden of stabilization on monetary policies. The costs of tight monetary policies have been high interest rates and restricted access to credit for the private sector. Small enterprises and farmers have been particularly hard hit.

In China, the government redirected the country's huge savings to the provinces by liberalizing agriculture and making coastal and economic zones attractive manufacturing platforms for export. The economic reform program emphasized gradual trade reform, exchange rate reform, and internal price deregulation. In India, the government's reform program focused on fiscal stability, with trade liberalization (particularly a reduction in the coverage of quantitative restrictions on imports) and deregulation of internal markets (including greater competition in the financial sector).

Fast and slow growers

Many low-income countries improved their economic performance after implementing these reform programs. Since the better performers included China, India, and other highly populated Asian countries, this economic growth improved the living standards of more than 2 billion people. But many low-income countries did not enjoy better economic performance because reforms were minimal or because the supply response stimulated by new incentives was constrained by structural and institutional weaknesses and by deficiencies in physical infrastructure and human resources. The variation across countries—in GDP growth, in savings and investment, in export growth and diversification, and in the reduction of poverty—has been enormous.

GDP growth

Real GDP growth for low-income countries as a whole was 5.1 percent a year during 1987–93, with real per capita growth of 3.1 percent a year—significantly higher than the 3.4 percent and 1.3 percent for other developing countries. But the low-income country average was pulled up by rapid growth in East Asia and the Pacific and, to a lesser extent, in South Asia (figures 1.1 and 1.2). China, driven by high rates of savings and investment and by solid export growth and diversification, recorded the strongest growth in real GDP and per capita GDP (9.3 percent and 7.8 percent a year) during 1987–93, while India, Pakistan, Sri Lanka, and Viet Nam grew between 4.0 and 7.5 percent a year.

Between 1988 and 1993, nearly half the countries in Sub-Saharan Africa achieved positive per capita GDP growth, a quarter with rates above the 1 to 2

FIGURE 1.1 REAL GDP GROWTH IN LOW-INCOME COUNTRIES

- **China** races ahead to catch middle-income countries within a generation—**other East Asian** countries follow
- **South Asia** picks up, but per capita growth rate is still between one-third and one-half of China's
- **Reforming Africa** recovers, but real per capita growth remains too small to dent poverty—**other African** countries regress

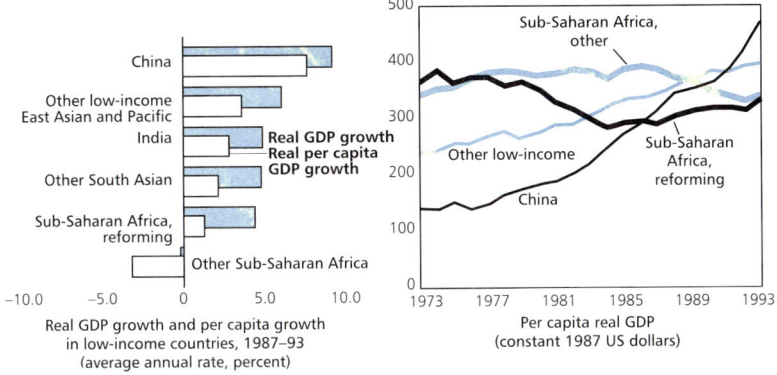

Real GDP growth and per capita growth
in low-income countries, 1987–93
(average annual rate, percent)

Per capita real GDP
(constant 1987 US dollars)

FIGURE 1.2 REAL PER CAPITA GDP GROWTH
IN LOW-INCOME COUNTRIES

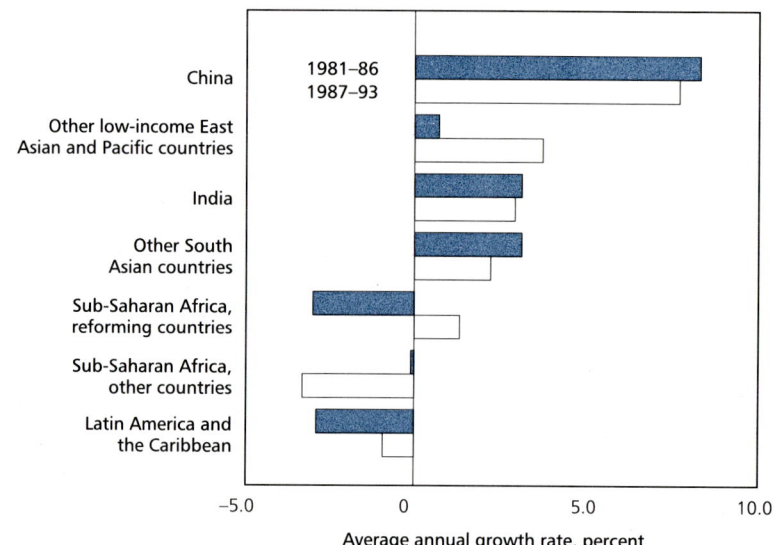

Source: World Bank data.

percent target set in the report, *Sub-Saharan Africa: From Crisis to Sustainable Growth—A Long-Term Perspective Study* (World Bank 1989; also known as the LTPS). The other half, some beset by social and political unrest, had negative growth rates. But even the worst performers in Sub-Saharan Africa performed better than the transition economies in Eastern Europe and Central Asia, where per capita incomes plunged 10 percent a year and more in the face of economic and political revolution, followed in several cases by civil unrest.

Sub-Saharan Africa's poor economic performance meant a deterioration in living standards for many and an increase in the number of absolute poor, from 184 million in 1985 to 216 million in 1990 (table 1.1). With 48 percent of its people impoverished, Africa is second only to South Asia in terms of absolute poverty. The growth in per capita income has been small because of Africa's rapidly growing population. Labor productivity, the key to increasing incomes, remains low. And in contrast to India and Pakistan, where faster growth was based on an increase in domestic savings, growth and investment in many African countries were driven by external assistance.

There also has been considerable variation across sectors within countries (figure 1.3). For most low-income countries, growth in real GDP during 1987–93 came more from industry and services (especially commerce) than

TABLE 1.1 POVERTY IN THE DEVELOPING WORLD, 1985 AND 1990

Region	Population (millions)		Number of poor (millions)		Headcount index[a] (percent)		Poverty gap index[b] (percent)	
	1985	1990	1985	1990	1985	1990	1985	1990
East Asia	1,379	1,496	182	169	13.2	11.3	3.3	2.8
China	1,049	1,133	108	128	10.3	11.3	2.2	3.1
Eastern Europe	70	70	5	5	7.1	7.1	2.4	1.9
Latin America and the Caribbean	388	429	87	108	22.4	25.2	8.7	10.3
Middle East and North Africa	196	221	60	73	30.6	33.1	13.2	14.3
South Asia	1,027	1,147	532	562	51.8	49.0	16.2	13.7
India	765	848	421	448	55.0	52.8	17.6	14.5
Sub-Saharan Africa	387	452	184	216	47.6	47.8	18.1	19.1
Total	3,446	3,815	1,051	1,133	30.5	29.7	9.9	9.5

a. Ratio of the number of poor to the total population.
b. Mean distance below the poverty line (zero for the nonpoor) as a percentage of the poverty line.
Source: Chen, Ravallion, and Datt 1993.

from agriculture. This was not the case for the reforming economies in Sub-Saharan Africa, where the larger contribution of agriculture to growth reflected liberalized agricultural producer prices and marketing arrangements and lower taxes on agricultural production and exports in the second half of the decade. African countries that made large improvements in their macroeconomic policies had stronger growth in the industrial sector (mining and petroleum and small industry and services in particular). It is encouraging that many reforming countries have been able to raise their agricultural growth rates close to those of China and other rapidly growing Asian economies; the challenge is for them to emulate the Asian developing economies by converting the fruits of increased agricultural growth into broader growth and development. But for most Sub-Saharan African countries and other low-income countries outside Asia, annual growth in agricultural output during 1987–93 still fell short of population growth.

Investment and savings

Divergent GDP growth rates in low-income countries match wide differences in their investment rates (figure 1.4). In East Asian countries, particularly

FIGURE 1.3 GROWTH IN AGRICULTURE, INDUSTRY, AND SERVICES
IN LOW-INCOME COUNTRIES, 1987–93

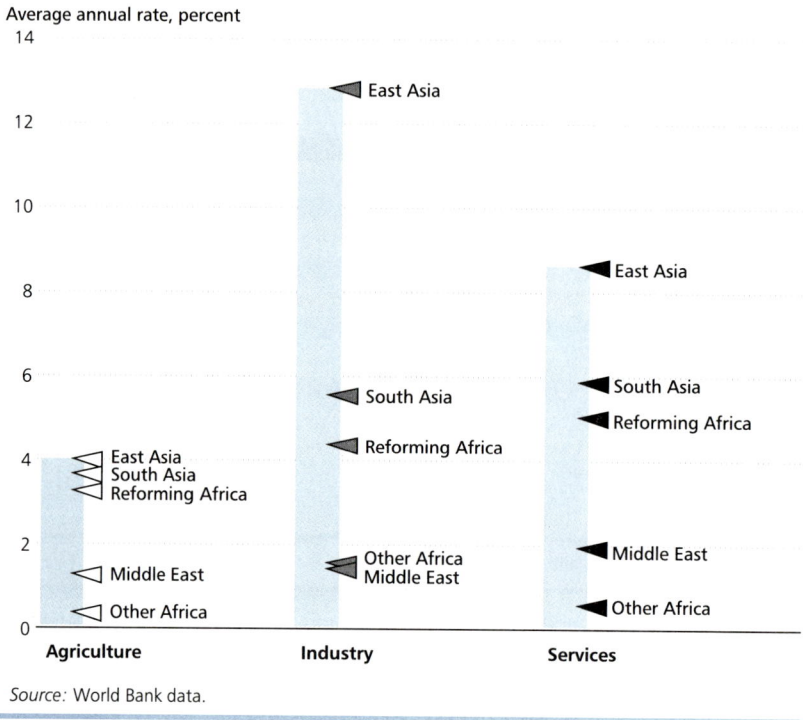

Source: World Bank data.

China, the investment-GDP ratio rose markedly and remained high during
1987–93. Low-income countries in East Asia have been investing more than a
third of GDP over the past decade. Rapid growth follows such high rates of
accumulation—even with large, continual leakages to public enterprises, as in
China where the leakages are 3–5 percent of GDP. Most low-income countries
in South Asia have maintained investment rates around 20 percent of GDP
throughout the past decade. But in Sub-Saharan Africa, the ratios rose only
marginally, languishing around 16 percent of GDP, below what is needed for
sustainable long-term growth, although a few strong reforming countries raised
investment close to the 25 percent target of the LTPS. Fueled by expanding
official aid flows, the increase in investment in reforming countries was driven
by a recovery in government investment. The main reason for the limited
increase was the low level of private investment.

The impact of investment on growth depends not only on levels of accumulation but also on the efficiency of investment. Measures of efficiency for
low-income countries show the same variation as growth rates and investment.

FIGURE 1.4 GROSS DOMESTIC INVESTMENT IN LOW-INCOME
COUNTRIES

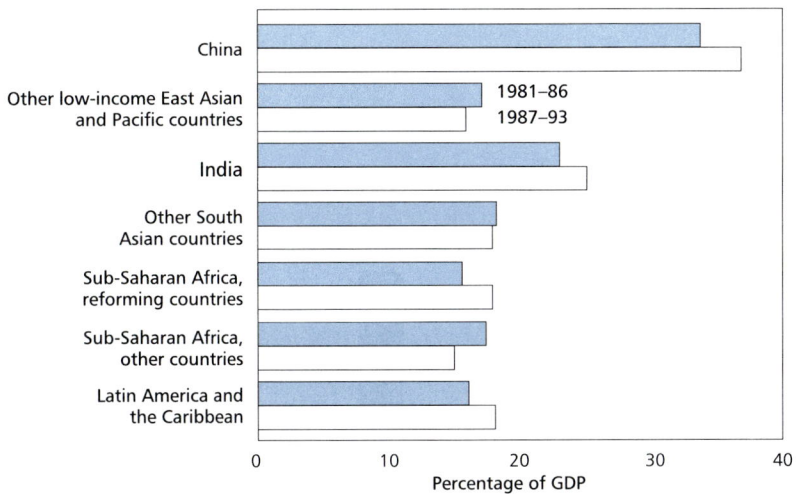

Source: World Bank data.

But the correlation is strong between rates of accumulation and efficiency of
investment—a strong rate of accumulation has been matched by low incre-
mental capital-output ratios (ICORs). The ICORs of most Sub-Saharan African
countries have been consistently higher—reflecting lower efficiency—than
those in Asian low-income countries.

China maintained a high gross savings rate, at 39 percent of GDP, during
1987–93. In Sub-Saharan Africa, though, savings rates have been low (figure
1.5), and the worst performers have even had negative savings. The reforming
countries increased savings to finance an increase in investment and to narrow
their external current account deficit. But few countries in Africa have reached
15 percent, let alone the 18 percent savings target in the LTPS. The poor showing in gross savings in Africa has generally been caused by government dissaving, reflecting the increased burden of state-owned enterprises on the
budget and difficulties in restraining public expenditure growth and raising tax
revenues. The limited success of many low-income Sub-Saharan countries in
containing fiscal pressures increased their recourse to the financial system,
crowding out the private sector.

Exports

Export performance has also varied widely among low-income countries (figure 1.6). China's export growth was striking: total exports reached $85 billion

FIGURE 1.5 GROSS DOMESTIC SAVINGS IN LOW-INCOME COUNTRIES

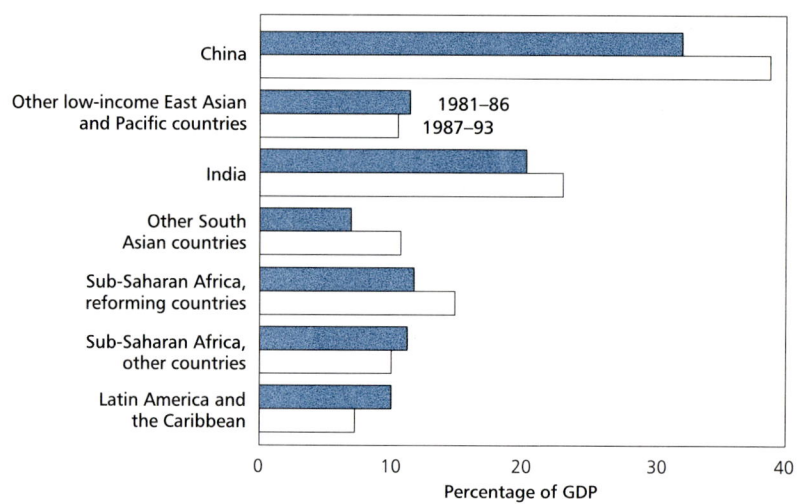

Source: World Bank data.

FIGURE 1.6 MERCHANDISE EXPORTS

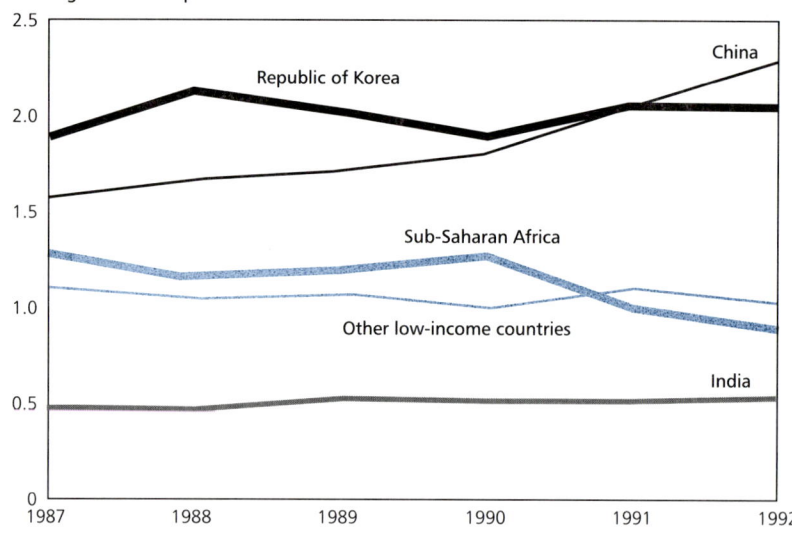

Source: World Bank data.

in 1992 and accounted for 2.3 percent of total world exports (China's exports rose to $101 billion in 1993). In India, while exports have registered double-digit growth rates over the past two years in response to economic reforms, the export base is still relatively undiversified and dependent on a few categories of consumer goods—such as gems, jewelry, and ready-made cotton garments. India will soon reach market saturation in gems and jewelry unless it upgrades its technology to cut and polish higher-value diamonds. And in ready-made cotton garments, growth has occurred through better use of textile quotas being phased out under the Uruguay Round. Maintaining current export growth rates and long-term competitiveness will require diversifying exports and making substantial investments to improve productivity and efficiency across a broad range of manufacturing industries, as was done in the East Asian economies.

Sub-Saharan Africa's share of world exports declined from about 1.3 percent in 1987 to less than 1 percent in 1992, while the market shares of other

TABLE 1.2 AVERAGE SHARE OF PRIMARY COMMODITIES IN EXPORT EARNINGS OF SUB-SAHARAN AFRICAN COUNTRIES, 1990–93

(percent)

Coffee		Cotton		Diamonds	
Uganda	70.6	Chad	49.5	Cen. African Rep.	53.4
Burundi	66.7	Mali	48.2	Sierra Leone	17.7
Rwanda	59.3	Burkina Faso	31.9	Zaire	12.1
Ethiopia	52.5	Sudan	25.2	Guinea	10.0
Equatorial Guinea	39.4	Zimbabwe	20.5		
Tanzania	20.3	Tanzania	19.6	**Aluminum**	
Kenya	15.3	Togo	18.0	Sierra Leone	19.8
Madagascar	10.9			Guinea	19.0
Cocoa		**Timber**		**Copper**	
São Tomé	80.2	Central African Rep.	18.8	Zambia	80.4
Ghana	32.9	Ghana	12.6	Zaire	44.7
Côte d'Ivoire	30.5				
Tea		**Fish**		**Petroleum**[a]	
Kenya	27.5	Mauritania	53.0	Nigeria	94.2
Rwanda	24.4	Mozambique	38.8	Congo	83.2
Burundi	12.8	Senegal	22.4	Angola	77.1
Malawi	9.5			Cameroon	48.1

a. Data are for 1985–87.
Source: World Bank data.

low-income countries remained constant. Africa's export growth was concentrated in a small number of countries: Côte d'Ivoire, Ethiopia, Gabon, Ghana, Kenya, Mozambique, Nigeria, Tanzania, and Uganda. And it came mainly from an increase in export volumes of primary commodities, which still account for about 89 percent of Africa's exports. Moreover, many Sub-Saharan African countries are very dependent on one or a few commodities for most of their export revenues (table 1.2). Continued concentration in primary commodity exports keeps low-income countries vulnerable to external shocks, particularly changes in world commodity prices. With the exception of primary commodities, export ratios in Africa's low-income countries remain extremely low, especially in manufacturing. However, a few countries, such as Kenya and Madagascar, are now diversifying into nontraditional exports such as horticulture and agro-based manufacturing (box 1.1).

Foreign direct investment

The experience of the Asian economies shows that foreign direct investment (FDI) can accelerate the rate of growth and diversification of exports—not only by providing finance but also by giving access to technology and markets. In China, FDI increased from a trickle in the early 1980s to $7.2 billion in 1992 and $20.0 billion in 1993. Firms benefiting from foreign investments accounted for $36 billion, or 36 percent, of the country's exports in 1993 (box 1.2). In

---

BOX 1.1 EXPORTS OF KENYAN FRESH VEGETABLES: THE IMPORTANCE OF NETWORKING

Among developing countries, Kenya has some of the longest standing and most diversified fresh vegetable exports to Western Europe. Pioneered in 1957, the vegetable trade has expanded since the 1970s. Exports increased from $2.3 million in 1970 to $47.7 million in 1987–89. Exports cater mainly to the niche market for "Asian vegetables" consumed by Asian ethnic communities in Europe. During the 1980s, despite increased competition from European and Mediterranean countries, Kenyan exporters managed to obtain price premiums for quality, maintain market share, and penetrate distribution channels of supermarket chains. Exports grew because leading producers, of Asian origin, exploited ethnic and family ties in buying countries, and because of a major increase in available air-freight space, enabling exporters to provide vegetables year-round while competitors had a shorter growing season. Over the past decade, Kenyan exporters have diversified into products such as tropical fruit and cut flowers. The industry has grown from a handful of medium-size and large producers to thousands of smallholders, providing an important source of income and employment to many people.

India foreign investment amounted to $4.7 billion in 1993, with a sharp increase f $4.1 billion in portfolio investment. Foreign direct investment increased to about $452 million in Pakistan in 1993. Sub-Saharan Africa has had limited success in attracting investment, and many countries have been wary of efforts to promote it. Of worldwide flows of $200 billion a year, the region received only $693 million in 1993 (figure 1.7). Indeed, there is increasing concern that, outside mining and petroleum, there has been considerable foreign disinvestment from Africa, reflecting the uncertain economic environ-

---

BOX 1.2 UNLEASHING THE PRIVATE SECTOR: FDI AND EXPORT GROWTH IN CHINA

China's record of sustained reform attracted a massive increase in foreign direct investment (FDI), which grew from a trickle in the early 1980s to $7.2 billion in 1992 and to more than $20.0 billion in 1993. Investment was initially concentrated in tourism, commercial real estate, and petroleum. Close to half the FDI was in Fujian, Guangdong, and Jiangsu, where it accounted for between 50 and 60 percent of gross capital formation. This concentration of investment in the coastal zone was stimulated by local governments that had taken advantage of their administrative and policy freedom to build the infrastructure needed to attract foreign investment, to provide attractive tax deals to foreign investors, and to refrain from intruding in businesses or overburdening firms with regulation.

In recent years, nearly 80 percent of FDI has been in small and medium-scale export-oriented manufacturing industries, with the average investment increasing from $0.5 million in the late 1980s to $1.5 million in 1992. Most of the investment was by overseas Chinese who had already established strong links to the main export markets in Europe, Japan, and the

United States. As a result of this boom in export-oriented FDI, exports have become the main engine of growth for the Chinese economy, and the country has significantly increased its share of world trade. The share of exports in GDP grew from 10.4 percent in 1985 to 24.6 percent in 1992, and China's share of world trade increased from 1.5 percent to 2.3 percent during the same period.

FDI is now being more evenly distributed as more of the funds are moving to the eastern and northeastern areas. Included are investments in power, where China expects about $67 billion in new investment by 2000, and in the telecommunications, chemical, petrochemical, and automotive industries. Unlike the coastal areas, firms in the expanding regions face more difficult problems of inadequate infrastructure, bureaucratic controls, opaque rules and regulations, and an underdeveloped legal system. But the lure of China's large and growing market and the government's commitment to transforming China into a dynamic market economy is irresistible—and the entry of such large investments will help correct many of the structural weaknesses facing China today.

FIGURE 1.7 NET FOREIGN DIRECT INVESTMENT

(billions of dollars)

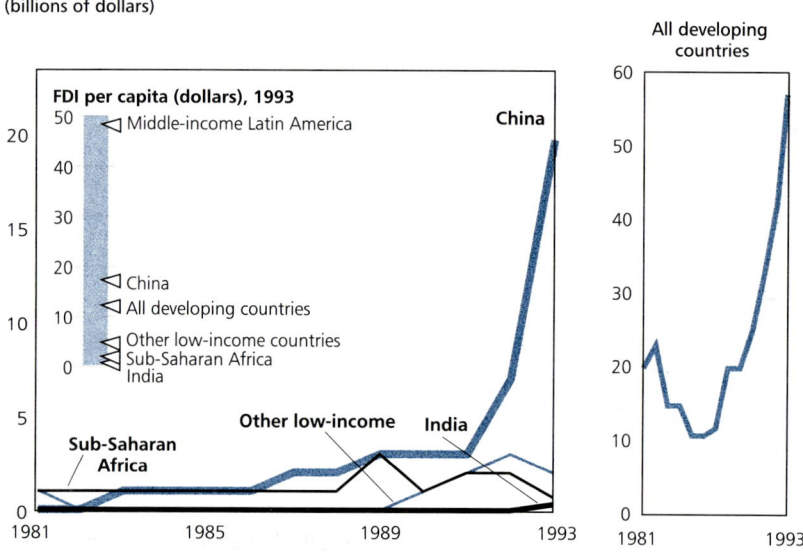

Source: International Monetary Fund data.

ment and growth prospects, the high cost of doing business, and the fears that policies and regulations discriminate against foreign investors.

Private sector–led growth

Growth in the better-performing low-income countries was led by the private sector. In China the reform program unleashed the pent-up energies of its people and added the capital, know-how, and connections of overseas Chinese and other foreigners. A large share of China's industrial growth came from foreign investors and from collectively owned enterprises (COEs), which were subject to competitive pressures similar to those facing the private sector. In India and Pakistan, now growing at a respectable 5 percent a year, the private sector has responded to trade liberalization, deregulation of the real and financial sectors, and a lowering of entry barriers in previously restricted industries.

In almost all Asian countries, the growth of the private sector has spurred the development of financial markets. Many private banks and nonbank financial institutions entered the market to serve the growing trade and investment needs of the private sector. Perhaps most important for building a constituency and consensus for reform, this growth was shared by a large group of people.

In reforming African countries, the private sector was the engine of growth—evident in the strong performance of the agricultural sector as well as the growth of small enterprises in industry and services.

Explaining differences in performance

What accounts for the large variation in performance across low-income countries and particularly in the strength of the private sector response to economic reforms? The reforms had their foundation in exchange rate reform—necessary but not sufficient for growth. In general, there has been a strong correlation between improvements in performance and the depreciation of the real effective exchange rate needed to compensate for worsening terms of trade (figure 1.8). Sub-Saharan African economies with fixed exchange rates lost competitiveness during the 1980s, since prices were inflexible downward. In contrast, Sub-Saharan African economies with flexible exchange rates engineered substantial depreciations of the real exchange rate—enough in most cases to eliminate black market premiums for foreign exchange. Movements of similar magnitude are observed for China and India.

However, the difference between China and India on the one hand and Sub-Saharan African economies on the other was that the latter increased growth rates by less than what the scale of real devaluation would suggest. Much of the explanation lies in their deficient infrastructure and human resource weaknesses, but also in public sector inefficiencies and losses, leakages from the financial system, and low saving and investment rates. These have compounded the deficiencies in the business environment that raise the cost of doing business. Insufficient transport, telecommunications, and other public utilities—and limited human and institutional capacities (low literacy rates and shortages of specialized business expertise in particular)—combine with low levels of savings to impose basic structural obstacles to rapid supply responses. These can be overcome only with time and sustained investment and support by governments.

The better-performing low-income countries have put in place more comprehensive and sustained reform programs—of macroeconomic stabilization, trade and tax reform, and internal market liberalization. By doing this, they conveyed to their people—and to the world—their commitment to developing market-oriented economies. They complemented trade liberalization with reforms to increase internal competition. And they started to put in place legal and regulatory systems and institutions supporting greater private involvement in the economy. As a result, the better performers got closer to achieving the "critical mass" of structural reforms necessary to improve the business environment and induce a significant supply response from the private sector.

Getting closer to the critical mass of structural reforms is part of the explanation of higher growth. But some high performers succeeded despite

FIGURE 1.8 REAL EFFECTIVE EXCHANGE RATES AND TERMS OF TRADE

(1980=100)

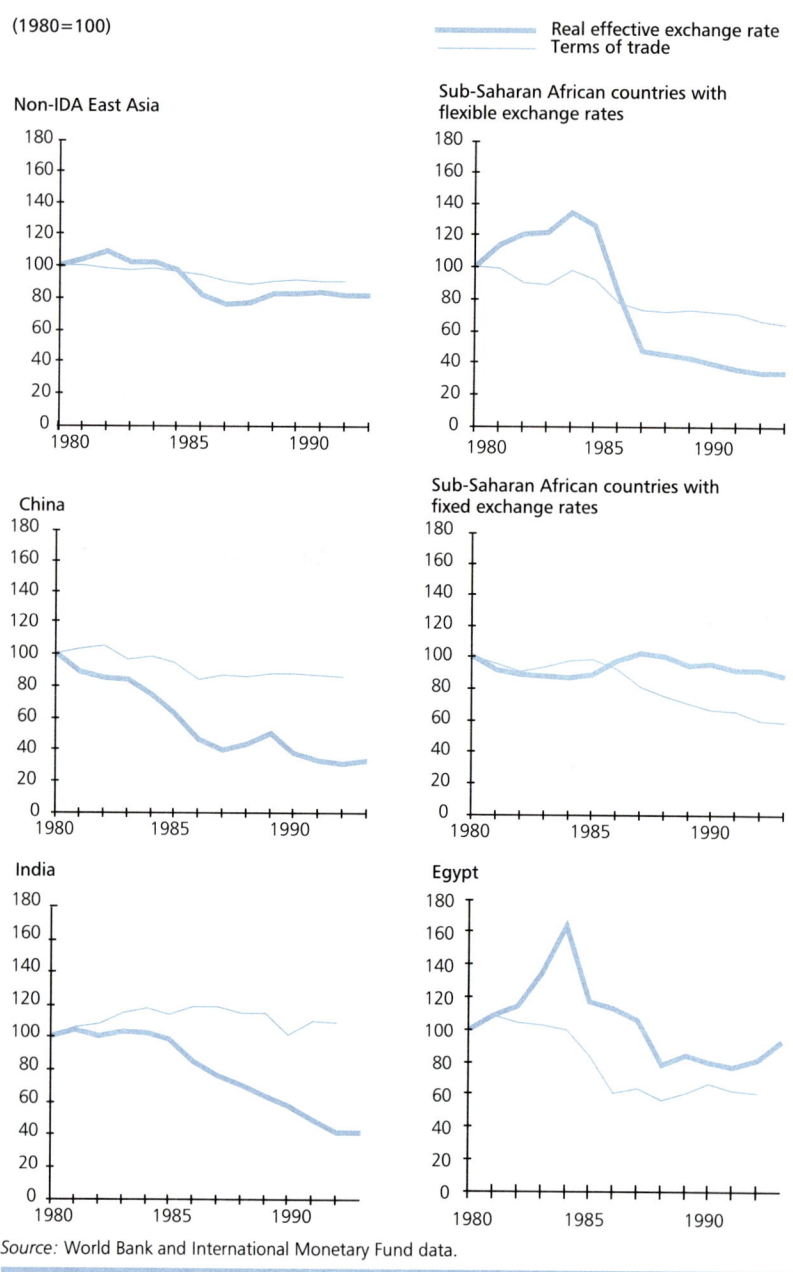

Source: World Bank and International Monetary Fund data.

shortcomings in their policy and institutional frameworks. The key difference was in their high savings rates. Countries with high domestic savings, such as China and India, enjoyed substantial benefits as sizable fractions of domestic savings and investment were allocated more efficiently, despite gradual and often partial structural reforms. While macroeconomic imbalances could and did occur in these countries as a result of fiscal slippage in India and the fiscal drain of state-owned enterprises (SOEs) in China, solutions have been more under their control. There was a reasonable degree of confidence among domestic and foreign investors that macroeconomic balance was achievable, based on the countries' efforts and track records.

In the low performers, mainly in Africa where partial reforms were insufficient to support sustained growth, chronically low or nonexistent domestic savings and very low investment made the impact of any structural reforms much more limited and slow-working. Sizable public sector losses and major expenditures on a large and inefficient civil service—the two main causes of fiscal instabilities—have also contributed to the stop-and-go reforms characterizing many African economies. Moreover, their heavy dependence on foreign aid flows presented a dilemma. Aid was crucial to maintain investment at levels required to achieve growth and poverty reduction. But at the same time, the dependence on aid tended to put a serious damper on domestic and foreign investors' confidence. Given low domestic private savings, and aid flows supporting public rather than private investment, the pool of investable resources for private sector development was limited, making private sector–led growth slow (and easily reversible).

To accelerate private sector–led growth, low-income countries need to move farther and faster to complete the agenda of structural reforms. But for the poorest performers (and their donors), the challenge is greater, and the risks of failure higher. To provide the resources for private sector development as well as for needed public investments, they must raise domestic savings—a process that will take time. In the meantime, putting in place a comprehensive package of reforms and maintaining it over time is particularly important for creating conditions for increased private savings and investment. If some crucial element is missing, progress is likely to be limited and easily reversible— these countries cannot afford the luxury of a partial approach and have less margin for error and delay.

Problems of political economy only complicate the picture—with low levels of income and human resource development, a history of ethnic problems, and weak political and civic institutions. Maintaining the political stability and commitment required to get on a virtuous circle is much more difficult.

The remainder of this chapter looks in more detail at three areas that will need to be addressed to raise domestic savings and private sector investment in low-income countries. First are the fiscal drain of public enterprises, the leakages from the financial sector, and the efficiency costs imposed by public enterprises. Second are barriers to internal and external competition and the harsh business environment faced by the private sector. Third is the poor quality of infrastructure and human resources.

The drag of public enterprises

Recent policy reforms in many low-income countries have failed to reduce significantly the dominance of the public sector in the economy. The inefficiency of public enterprises and the spread of their losses throughout the economy continue to drag down savings, investment, and economic growth.

The dominance of the public sector

In most low-income countries, the public sector is dominant in infrastructure, heavy industry, agricultural marketing, and finance—typically accounting for more than 10 percent of GDP, 20 percent of employment, and 25 percent of investment. But public enterprises account on average for 14 percent of GDP, 18 percent of employment, and 27 percent of investment in Sub-Saharan Africa. In many countries public enterprises have retained their shares of production and employment even after public sector reform. This persistence reflects continuing investment in public enterprises as well as the slow pace and limited scope of divestiture. With few exceptions, divestiture programs in low-income countries have consisted mainly of privatization or liquidation of small enterprises, with little impact on the structure or performance of the economy.

Public enterprises dominate large industry, especially in Asia. In China, state-owned enterprises are particularly dominant in capital goods, such as steel, machinery-building, cement, and energy production, despite the growth of COEs and private firms during the past decade. This pattern also holds in other Asian economies that historically have adopted a mixed economy approach. In India, the public sector owns 50 percent of industrial assets, mainly in heavy industry, and accounts for 25 percent of industrial production. In Pakistan, the integrated steel works is publicly owned, while the private sector owns small arc furnaces, foundries, and ship-breaking. In the heavy engineering sector, large state enterprises in machine-building and machine tools exist alongside private engineering firms.

Agricultural development is still circumscribed by heavy state intervention, mainly through direct involvement in the marketing of inputs, outputs, and support services. The inefficiencies of these institutions have muted the supply response of the agricultural sector since increases in the price of tradables resulting from exchange rate reform often have not been fully passed through to producers. Even when marketing systems have been liberalized, private sector entry has been limited because of restrictive and discretionary licensing systems and the limited, high-cost credit provided by a state-dominated financial system.

The dominance of public enterprises in the economies of low-income countries means, when they perform poorly, that they drag down overall growth rates. In Kenya, for instance, total factor productivity in majority-owned state enterprises declined 3 percent during 1986–91, compared with a 5 percent increase in the private sector. If state enterprises had been as productive as the private sector during this period, Kenya's GDP would have grown by an additional 2 percent each year. Public enterprise inefficiency has an even larger impact in countries with more dominant public sectors than Kenya's.

The dominance of public enterprises in the economies of low-income countries means, when they perform poorly, that they drag down overall growth rates

---

For private firms, the inefficiency of public enterprises raises the cost of doing business. In Sub-Saharan Africa, the poor quality of utilities and infrastructure services adds 10–25 percent to firms' costs. It has been estimated that the efficiency losses of the publicly owned petroleum sector in Sub-Saharan Africa amount to about $1.4 billion a year (box 1.3)—more than the Bank's annual disbursement of adjustment policy loans to the region, and about two times the foreign direct investment in 1993.

Fiscal drain and financial sector leakages

The losses of unprofitable public enterprises are typically financed by a combination of transfers from the fiscal budget, a tax on the financial system through forced investments and portfolio requirements, and domestic credit, which increases the cost and reduces the volume of credit to the private sector. Public enterprise losses often are large relative to the size of low-income economies and reduce the availability of resources to finance private sector activity as well as alternative public investments. Often, the lack of data on state-owned enterprises, their losses, and the distribution of those losses throughout the economy makes it even more difficult to deal with them.

Covering public enterprise losses with fiscal transfers forces governments to finance larger fiscal deficits and increase tax revenues or reduce public expenditures in other areas, or both. Increasing tax revenues to finance the losses of state enterprises is difficult in many low-income countries, where the tax base is narrow and tax administration weak. During the 1980s most reforming low-

---

**BOX 1.3 THE HIGH COST OF INEFFICIENT PUBLIC ENTERPRISES:
PETROLEUM IN SUB-SAHARAN AFRICA**

Oil products in Sub-Saharan Africa represent 70 percent of total commercial energy consumption, consume one-third of available hard currency reserves, and account for two-fifths of indirect taxes.

The petroleum products industry in Sub-Saharan Africa is extremely inefficient. A 1992 study estimated total annual potential savings of more than $1.4 billion (approximately $51 a ton). The scale of these efficiency losses can be gauged from the facts that they exceeded IDA's total disbursements in that year to Sub-Saharan Africa for adjustment programs and they were twice the FDI inflows.

The key areas of inefficiency:

■ *Procurement ($690 million).* Most countries suffer from lack of foreign exchange and from monopolistic and inefficient government involvement in procurement.

■ *Refining ($550 million).* Most refineries are too small, lack adequate technology, and face inadequate incentives for efficiency improvements.

■ *Distribution ($180 million).* Transportation infrastructure is run-down.

The study indicated that more than half the estimated savings could be achieved without new investments—by changing policies and procedures, particularly opening markets to competition and providing adequate pricing policies, and by regional cooperation. The key investment requirements would be for rationalizing and rehabilitating transport and storage facilities.

---

income countries reduced their budget deficits by cutting spending rather than by increasing revenues. Faced with strong political pressures, governments often sacrificed public investments with long-term benefits—including social and infrastructure investments—rather than cut current expenditures. In Sub-Saharan Africa, for example, average capital expenditures fell from 8.7 percent of GDP to 6.1 percent during the 1980s.

Governments in low-income countries often have controlled interest rates to reduce the fiscal cost of accommodating budget deficits. But reduced real deposit rates, often negative, have been a disincentive to savings (encouraging savers to seek nonfinancial assets), fostered capital flight, and encouraged overborrowing by enterprises. As a result, financial depth is shallower in low-income countries than in other economies. This is especially true in Sub-Saharan Africa, where bank deposits are only 15–20 percent of GDP (compared with 40 percent in Pakistan, 60 percent in India, and 80 percent in China).

The financing of state enterprise losses through the domestic financial sector—directly, through credit to state enterprises, or indirectly, through credit to the government to finance budget transfers—increases the cost and reduces the availability of credit to the private sector. In Africa, the public share of domestic bank credit averages around 40 percent and exceeds 80 percent in some countries. In countries where banks are required to invest a certain portion of their assets in government paper or other forced investments at below-market returns, the effect is a tax on the financial sector that is usually reflected in higher intermediation margins. Even in countries that do not require banks to invest in particular industries, the allocation of credit often is not fully market-determined. Where state-owned banks dominate the financial sector, as they do in most low-income countries, they often channel resources to public enterprises rather than act as independent financial intermediaries. In addition, where the public sector is a dominant force in the real sectors, banks are under continual pressure to lend to public enterprises to prop up the banks' own non-performing assets and to prop up their client firms that are linked with state enterprises (figure 1.9).

In many low-income countries, state enterprise losses are so large that they are two to three times public expenditures on education and health. Typically, a majority of these losses is attributable to a relatively small number of large state-owned enterprises. These normally are utilities (power, telecommunications, water, railways, ports), capital-intensive industries (steels, fertilizers, chemicals, pulp and paper, cement), and agricultural marketing boards. The fiscal drain of public enterprise losses is a form of continual government dissaving that makes it difficult for low-income countries to generate the total savings

FIGURE 1.9 PUBLIC ENTERPRISES CROWD OUT PRIVATE CREDIT, 1986–88

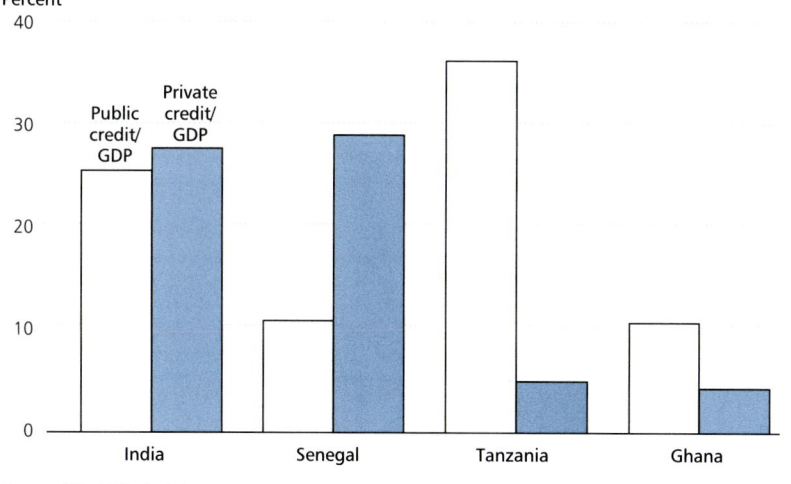

Source: World Bank data.

needed for accumulation and growth. In Africa, the drain on the fiscal budget and the leakages from the financial system resulting from public enterprise losses can be as high as 12 percent of GDP, nearly as great as gross domestic savings (averaging 12.5 percent) and two to three times the spending on health and education. So, few resources remain for investment, public or private.

In China, fiscal losses of SOEs (that is, not counting losses in the banking system) are 3–5 percent of GDP. They are less significant in crowding out investment since gross savings have been about 39 percent during 1987–93. Still, accommodating such losses threatens the viability of the financial system, where it is estimated that 15–20 percent of the loans of state banks are nonperforming. The fast-growing economies would thus have done better but for the drag of the public sector on savings and investment.

Regulation and barriers to competition— a harsh business environment

Although reforming countries have taken significant steps to improve the business environment, private sector development in many low-income countries is still discouraged by a harsh business environment that increases the cost and risk of doing business—often hitting small and medium-size firms the hardest. Even informal sector firms are not exempt, for they benefit from freedom from regulation at the cost of being excluded from opportunities participation in the formal sector could bring. And despite considerable progress in trade liberalization, further progress is still required. True, many low-income countries have reduced the coverage of nontariff barriers and rationalized tariff codes. But many have not yet introduced low or moderate tariffs, in part because of the continuing importance of tariffs for government revenues.

The result is a continuing bias against exports and a high cost for inputs. Making things worse, marketing boards continue to be heavily involved in agricultural exports in most African countries.

Further trade reform must be accompanied by legal, regulatory, and institutional reforms. Increasingly, the emphasis on improving the business environment needs to swing toward the wide range of legal, regulatory, and institutional deficiencies that are only now being addressed in most countries' reform programs.

In many low-income countries, internal competition—and thus the capacity of domestic firms to respond to external competition—has been limited by incomplete price liberalization, licensing requirements, and special concessions. These policies create barriers to the entry of private sector firms and insulate firms from competitive pressures to innovate, reduce costs, and seek new markets. Such policies also tend to preserve the rents received by privileged firms, discriminating in particular against small and medium-size enterprises.

One major obstacle to creating competitive markets is the presence of public enterprises in key sectors of the economy. Public enterprises tend to deter private entry, in part because they enjoy privileges not available to private firms, such as tax exemptions, access to government contracts, immunity from normal commercial law, and so on. The small markets in many low-income countries mean that public enterprises may enjoy a monopoly, particularly in nontraded goods industries. Even where such state monopolies have been abolished, state enterprises often retain privileges that deter private producers and traders.

In addition to improving the capacity of the private sector to respond to improvements in incentives for production and investment, deregulation of the economy in turn has an important impact on the public sector. It reduces the administrative burden on public services and redirects the efforts of government toward areas that help firms to exploit market opportunities and develop technological, management, and marketing skills to improve their productivity. Issues relating to improvement of the business environment are discussed in chapter 2.

Poor quality of physical infrastructure and human resources

Physical infrastructure services—power, transport, roads, civil works, telecommunications, water, sanitation, and waste disposal—represent a significant share of every economy, typically 7 to 11 percent of GDP, with transport the largest. They are not only important consumption goods, as with clean water and electricity for households, but also vital inputs into the production process, as with power, transport to markets, and communications with buyers and sellers. Provision of infrastructure services lags behind in low-income countries, severely hampering development efforts as well as welfare improvements.

The share of infrastructure services provided by state-owned utilities is much higher in low-income countries than elsewhere. The dominant public role, exercised largely through vertically integrated and monolithic entities, has arisen for a combination of reasons: technological characteristics, economic and political importance, and scale of financial requirements, as well as high levels of uncertainty and risk that have deterred private investment. Provision of infrastructure services in low-income countries presents common problems—operational inefficiency, overstaffing, poor maintenance, and an inability to meet rapidly increasing demands for new infrastructure.

Inefficiencies in the provision of physical infrastructure are quickly felt throughout the economy because of their impact on the costs of doing business. In Nigeria, power shortages have induced most large private enterprises to install their own electricity generators, increasing total machinery and equipment costs by 10 to 25 percent. Inefficiencies and shortages also restrict access to markets. Neglect of rural infrastructure in particular has slowed the integration of rural and urban markets and cut off farmers from inputs at competitive prices. Moreover, lack of access to new technology, especially in telecommunications and transport, erodes the competitiveness of both rural and urban producers.

Low-income countries are also characterized by widespread deficiencies in human resources, which are the key to long-term competitiveness. While many countries have improved their social indicators—enrollment ratios in primary and secondary education, literacy ratios, access to clean water and sanitation, life expectancy at birth, and infant mortality rates—they continue to lag behind middle-income countries, especially in Sub-Saharan Africa (figures 1.10, 1.11, and 1.12).

Low-income countries are also characterized by widespread deficiencies in human resources and infrastructure services, which are the keys to long-term competitiveness

Adult illiteracy rates remain high, especially for females, in most of Sub-Saharan Africa and Asia. There are exceptions, such as China, Kenya, Madagascar, Myanmar, and Sri Lanka, where literacy rates are relatively high for both males and females. The link between literacy and productivity improvements is strong, and experience has demonstrated the difficulty of imparting information about technologies, markets, and so on to an illiterate population. In addition, the relatively high rates of female illiteracy in most low-income countries are significant for private sector development—because women are major actors in the informal sector and agriculture, and because public extension services and other agencies relevant to business development typically focus their activities on males.

Some countries where illiteracy remains high, such as India, now have relatively high primary and secondary enrollment ratios—the result of efforts to improve the quality of human capital. But in most Sub-Saharan African countries, primary and secondary enrollments have grown relatively slowly and still lag well behind those in other developing countries. Indeed, between 1985 and 1990 primary enrollment fell as a percentage of all those eligible to attend primary school—a most troubling development. Moreover, while the share of outlays on education in total government expenditure in Sub-Saharan Africa has increased—in 1989, the average was 4.1 percent of GDP, on par with many middle-income countries—African governments have been less successful than those elsewhere in shifting spending toward primary and secondary education.

FIGURE 1.10 ADULT LITERACY RATES IN LOW-INCOME COUNTRIES, 1992

Percentage of population age 15 and over

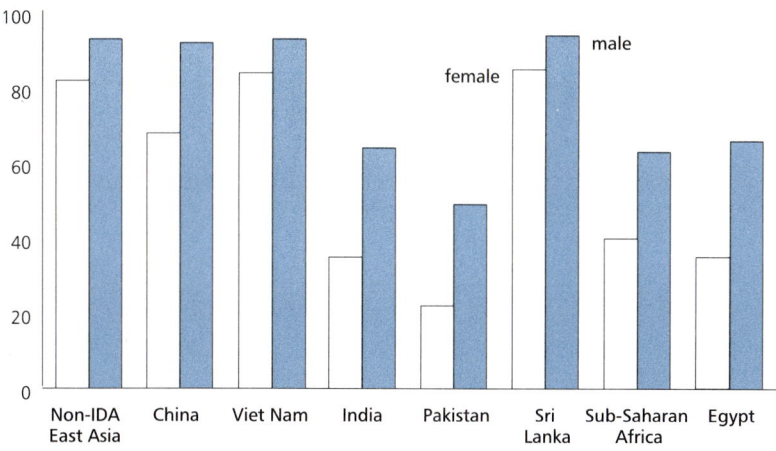

Source: United Nations Development Programme data.

FIGURE 1.11 SCHOOL ENROLLMENTS IN LOW-INCOME COUNTRIES, 1990

Percentage of age group enrolled

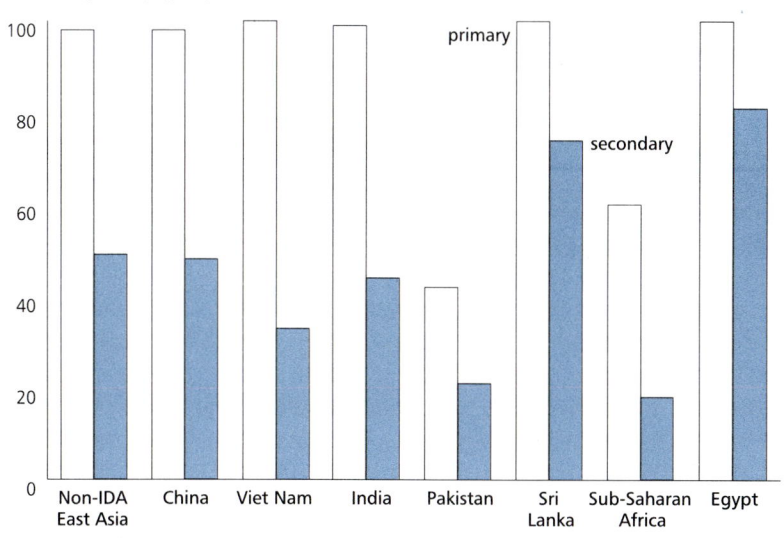

Source: United Nations Development Programme data.

FIGURE 1.12 ACCESS TO SANITATION IN LOW-INCOME COUNTRIES, 1985–91

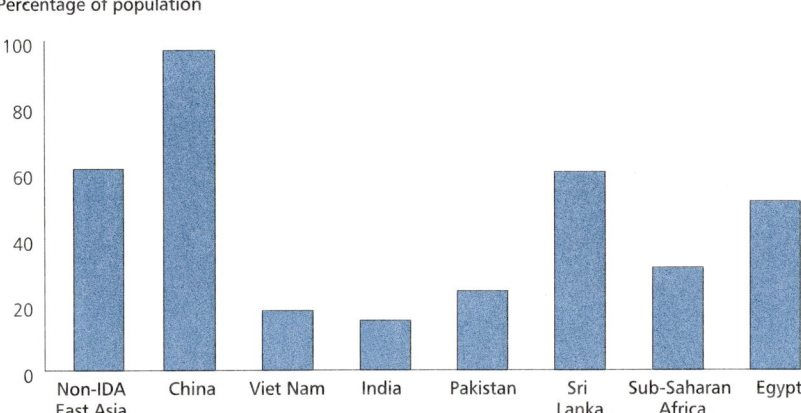

Percentage of population

Source: United Nations Development Programme data.

To support growth and poverty alleviation and promote the private sector, governments in low-income countries need to use the fiscal space created by public enterprise and tax reform to redirect spending toward infrastructure and human resources, subject to the first priority of maintaining fiscal stability. The challenge is not only to expand spending and increase its efficiency in these areas, but also to focus spending on essential public goods, such as transport, water, and primary and secondary education.

The reform agenda

With the severity of poverty and the speed of population growth in most low-income countries, even the respectable growth rates of the successful performers are not enough. With population increases of 3 percent a year, a 4–5 percent GDP growth rate means per capita incomes will rise only 1–2 percent a year. At that rate it would take African countries more than half a century to join the ranks of middle-income countries. To reduce the number of poor, low-income countries must grow by 7–8 percent a year and ensure that the benefits of this faster growth reach the more than 1 billion people living in poverty. These high growth rates are also required to absorb the unemployed, new entrants into labor markets, and those made redundant by public enterprise and civil service reforms.

The key to accelerated growth is much higher investment and domestic savings, combined with systematic efforts to introduce structural reforms, which are necessary to maintain macroeconomic stability and stimulate the private sector. This is particularly true for the slow-growing economies, which need to raise savings and investment rates from the current 12–16 percent of GDP to at least 20–25 percent.

Raising the level and efficiency of investment requires further reforms to create a competitive, enabling environment for the private sector, to redirect financial resources to support private production and investment, and to shift the composition of public expenditures toward infrastructure and human resource investments that are essential for long-term sustained development. These reforms represent a fundamental change in the role of the state in the economy—from direct owner and operator to partner and regulator of the private sector.

Fostering competition means going faster and farther with trade reform and price deregulation

---

The agenda requires governments to:

Create a competitive yet attractive business environment. An efficient private sector–led development strategy means shifting from protecting domestic industry to making concerted efforts to reduce the cost of doing business—so that firms can compete in the global economy. To help firms respond quickly to changing market conditions, competent and agile institutions are needed—particularly those responsible for creating and enforcing legal and regulatory systems and tax and customs administration, and those dealing with trade, investment, and technology support. Fostering competition means going faster and farther with trade reform and price deregulation, removing remaining restrictions on FDI, and eliminating incentives and regulations that inhibit competition. By harnessing the skills and creativity of all segments of the population—including ethnic minorities and foreigners—the benefits of economic liberalization will support pluralistic societies. (Creating an attractive business environment and introducing an array of legal, regulatory, and institutional reforms are the subjects of chapter 2.)

Stop the hemorrhaging of public enterprises. Fiscal stability is fundamental to sustained growth. The key elements are broader tax bases and improved tax collections to increase fiscal revenues and, above all, reductions in government dissaving. For most countries, this means greater efforts to stem the losses of public enterprises—through privatization or, as an interim step, through the imposition of a hard budget constraint. As a first step, better information on state-owned enterprises is required to allow policies, programs, and performance targets to be defined. Privatization programs, beginning with the largest loss-makers, will have a bigger impact on the fiscal account and establish credibility for the overall program. Failure to deal with state enterprise losses will keep low-income countries from making social and infrastructure investments needed for growth and poverty alleviation. (These are the subjects of chapter 3.)

Increase the flow of financial resources to the private sector. The priority should be severing the links between banks and nonperforming assets. This means not only eliminating the leakages from the financial system to public enterprises and privileged firms, but also strengthening prudential supervision and regulation of the banking system. Reducing public sector ownership and promoting entry and competition will increase the volume and efficiency of financial intermediation. Removing impediments to private sector development in general will drive this process. At the same time, development of basic financial infrastructure—such as payment systems—is crucial. (Chapter 4 examines issues of financial sector development.)

Although all low-income countries share this reform agenda to some degree, their diversity—in initial conditions and the extent to which reforms are already completed or under way—means that priorities, sequencing, and implementation will vary.

The key to accelerated growth is much higher domestic savings and investment to reduce the dependence on aid flows

---

China's priority is to maintain its current growth rate and good macroeconomic management and to concentrate its efforts on integrating its segmented domestic market. Restructuring large public enterprises, building the financial sector, and strengthening the legal and regulatory frameworks are critical challenges. And large investments in infrastructure are needed to sustain growth.

For South Asia, the priorities are to reform tax systems, improve tax administration, accelerate the efforts to liberalize trade, deregulate the economy to increase internal competition, significantly reduce the cost of doing business, and accelerate the reform of public enterprises (particularly utilities) and the financial system.

In low-income countries with low domestic savings and low per capita GDP growth rates, including Bangladesh and most of Africa, the key to accelerated growth is much higher domestic savings and investment to reduce the dependence on aid flows. Reducing government dissaving in Africa will require a major change in the size and structure of public revenue and expenditure—by broadening the tax base, improving tax collections, and stopping the hemorrhaging of public enterprises. Increasing the flow of financial resources to the private sector will depend on cutting links between banks and nonperforming borrowers, privatizing banks, and strengthening prudential regulation and supervision.

Private sector development calls for a major effort to reduce the cost of doing business through deregulation to complement steady progress in trade reform. But private sector development is only one element of the development agenda. Complementary public investments in people, infrastructure, and the environment are essential. The emergence of a vibrant private sector will also hinge on a major sustained effort to develop competent, respected, and agile public institutions—a difficult and slow process.

Establishing an attractive business environment—agile firms, agile institutions

Commercial activity on the part of the ruler is harmful to his subjects and ruinous to the tax revenue...[it] crowds out competitors [and] dictates prices for materials and products which could lead to the financial ruin of many businesses. When the ruler's attacks on property are extensive and general, affecting all means of making a livelihood, the slackening of business activity too becomes general.

Ibn Khaldun, 14th century

THIS old truth is even more valid today. In a world where technological change is reducing transport costs, increasing global integration, and changing the nature of competition, firms can no longer compete on the basis of price alone. Design, quality, and timeliness of delivery are what gives today's firms a competitive edge. And for countries to compete successfully requires agile firms connected to world markets.

But firms in most low-income countries have been held back by a difficult business environment that has increased risks and transaction costs. While specific impediments vary, the consistent message is that competition is muted and firms are denied the means to respond to the changing competitive environment. They are denied by economic and political uncertainty, insecurity of economic rights, impediments to trade and investment, complex and discretionary regulations, and high costs of infrastructure and finance.

The private sector's assessment of the business environment

Several countries, often with help from the World Bank Group, have conducted surveys about how domestic and foreign private firms feel about the business environment (box 2.1). These surveys have produced a wealth of data about the costs enterprises face in starting, operating, and expanding their businesses and about how entrepreneurs rank various impediments to doing business:

- In Cameroon, firms have identified access to finance, lack of demand, and taxes and tax administration as the three most important constraints.
- Entrepreneurs in Côte d'Ivoire note the same constraints, adding political and policy uncertainty near the top of their list.
- In Kenya, entrepreneurs are concerned about macroeconomic stability, infrastructure, regulations, and access to finance.
- In Egypt, tax administration weighs almost as heavily on firms as taxes themselves. A business may not know its actual tax liability for ten years after submitting its declaration.
- In India, firms are burdened by excessive regulations that prevent them from responding to an increasingly competitive environment.
- In Sri Lanka, firms have identified the cost of finance, the level of taxes, poor infrastructure, labor regulations, and policy uncertainty as key constraints.

To compete successfully requires agile firms connected to world markets. But firms in most low-income countries have been held back by a difficult business environment that has increased risks and transaction costs

Private sector assessments and firm surveys suggest that these constraints can increase the cost of doing business by as much as 30 percent over costs in other countries. The surveys also suggest that when economic and political conditions are secure, when the risks of policy reversals are low, and when the business environment is inviting, domestic entrepreneurs are forthcoming in their investments, and foreign investors come in willingly.

Institutional Investor publishes biannual country credit ratings that reflect the international financial community's perception of the economic, financial, and political health of countries (table 2.1). In most low-income countries (except China and India), country risk is still perceived as high. Some countries, such as Bangladesh, Bolivia, Sri Lanka, Uganda, and Zambia, have improved their country credit ratings considerably. But most low-income

---

BOX 2.1 PRIVATE SECTOR ASSESSMENTS IN LOW-INCOME COUNTRIES:
A PARTICIPATORY APPROACH TO DIAGNOSIS AND IMPLEMENTATION

In collaboration with the governments and the private sector, IDA and IFC have prepared ten private sector assessments in low-income countries and are planning to complete eight more by the end of 1996. The assessments have:

■ Documented the private sector's economic role and its relation to the public sector.

■ Surveyed firms to improve the quality and quantity of data available regarding obstacles to private sector development—including insufficient access to credit and problems with starting, operating, and expanding a business.

■ Clarified issues related to the nature and sequencing of reforms affecting the private sector—such as macroeconomic and political stability and the functioning of financial markets.

■ Highlighted the high cost to business of complex regulations, poor infrastructure, and poor performance by public institutions—particularly institutions of public finance, such as customs and taxation.

■ Reduced mutual suspicion and stimulated constructive, focused dialogue between business and government—leading to the institutionalization of private-public consultative measures.

■ Helped the Bank Group to set priorities, define its agenda, and identify new projects in private sector development.

■ Helped coordinate donors' strategies and support for private sector development.

Based on the findings of past private sector assessments, the Bank Group is now focusing on developing standards for measuring the role of the private sector in the economy and defining constraints to private sector development arising from distorted incentives, excessive government regulations, crowding out by government, and weak support systems. Most important, private sector assessments are now being used to establish cooperative arrangements among the private sector, governments, the Bank Group, and the donor community to design reform programs acceptable to all key stakeholders.

---

countries need to make much greater efforts to overcome negative perceptions of country risk.

In Africa, the harsh business environment has generally resulted in poorer performance of private investment than in other parts of the world. Investments were most successful in countries where the business environment was hospitable. The IFC's operations in the export-oriented oil, gas, and mining sectors have performed well—because they have been structured to be insulated to a large degree from the local economy. But the performance of its investments in the manufacturing and service industries—when measured in financial and economic rates of return, specific loss reserves, and write-off rates—has been significantly below the average of these measures for the rest of the Corporation's portfolio. It is this latter category of investments whose performance is directly tied to the overall economic and business environment in the local economy.

Poor performance was rooted in macroeconomic shortcomings—mainly unrealistic exchange rates and foreign exchange shortages. Further increasing costs were infrastructure inadequacies that required firms to take on functions that private firms in other parts of the world did not have to be concerned with. And weakening the performance of investments were regulatory impediments—from price controls and import restrictions to interference in product mix decisions and labor markets and delays in granting permits.

In the past few years, many African governments have taken macroeconomic measures that are reducing the cost of doing business, and many have started the long process of correcting policy and institutional weaknesses that contribute to high risk and transaction costs. But much more needs to be done to change investors' perceptions.

China and India have demonstrated the value of economic reforms, particularly over the past four years. Their economic reforms have been rewarded

TABLE 2.1 COUNTRY CREDIT RATINGS

Country	1991	1994	1999
Switzerland	92.4	92.4	92.3
Malaysia	62.0	67.6	69.2
Thailand	62.5	62.2	62.8
China	53.1	57.4	58.4
India	38.4	42.2	46.2
Pakistan	27.0	29.7	30.1
Egypt	23.4	30.9	29.5
Sri Lanka	21.9	30.4	31.7
Zimbabwe	28.7	29.0	30.2
Ghana	N/A	27.6	29.2
Kenya	28.3	23.7	24.0
Bangladesh	16.4	23.2	25.0
Bolivia	15.0	21.4	23.2
Nigeria	19.5	18.4	17.6
Côte d'Ivoire	17.2	17.0	18.2
Tanzania	12.0	15.2	16.1
Zambia	9.8	13.9	14.4
Uganda	5.3	11.6	11.2
Zaire	10.1	8.3	7.5
Sierra Leone	6.9	7.4	5.8

Source: Institutional Investor, September 1991 and September 1994.

by expanded access to international capital markets and foreign direct investment (FDI), which has brought new markets, new technologies, and much-needed competition. In China, FDI went from negligible amounts at the beginning of the 1980s to nearly $20 billion in 1993. In India, FDI approvals went from $73 million in 1990 to more than $2 billion in 1993, and actual FDI flows increased from $165 million to $600 million. Indian firms have also raised more than $4 billion from international debt and equity markets.

Regaining the confidence of investors may take time. But once investments start, they create a virtuous cycle—investment flows increase the incentives to maintain stability and continuity, which in turn leads to more investments. The Multilateral Investment Guarantee Agency (MIGA) has been assisting low-income countries in starting this virtuous cycle by providing political risk insurance and technical assistance (box 2.2).

Foundations of a dynamic private sector

The emerging consensus of these surveys is that agile firms, which are necessary to compete in a rapidly changing environment, prosper when there is political and economic stability, when entrepreneurship and learning are rewarded, and when there is a commitment to shared growth. Creating this attractive environment requires a systematic, time-bound program formulated and implemented in collaboration with the private sector to put in place the underpinnings of a dynamic and competitive private sector (figure 2.1):

- Secure and flexible transactions, with the freedom, flexibility, and security to acquire, use, and leverage property rights (real, tangible, and intellectual).
- Nonintrusive, efficient, and respected public administration that sets widely understood rules for economic activity, enforces them uniformly and universally in a predictable manner, and changes them through transparent means.
- Competitive markets that promote mobility of products, capital, labor, and knowledge through simple, transparent, and uniformly applied incentive and regulatory systems.
- Efficient and responsive social, physical, and technological infrastructure that increases the long-term competitiveness of the economy and reduces transaction costs.

Building this structure is a difficult and time-consuming task. It implies a fundamental change in the role of the government, from owner and operator to policymaker and regulator working to develop a competitive, outward-looking economy in close partnership with the private sector. Fundamental to the success of this orientation is development of competent and agile institutions to support the rapid response of agile firms to changing market conditions. After

BOX 2.2 POLITICAL RISK, FOREIGN DIRECT INVESTMENT, AND MIGA

The Multilateral Investment Guarantee Agency (MIGA) was created to facilitate private foreign investment in developing member countries. By providing long-term noncancelable investment guarantees (insurance) to foreign investors against specified noncommercial risks—including currency transfer, expropriation, and war and civil disturbance—MIGA enables commercially attractive projects to proceed in many low-income countries. MIGA complements national and private investment insurance programs through coinsurance and reinsurance arrangements.

MIGA's guarantees, for investments as small as $150,000 and as large as $50 million in the infrastructure, mining, and financial sectors, have often been critical of the investor's decision to proceed with the project, including participating in privatization projects. As of January 1, 1995, MIGA has provided political risk insurance totaling $375 million in projects in eight low-income countries—Bangladesh, Cameroon, China, Honduras, Madagascar, Pakistan, Tanzania, and Uganda. Preliminary applications for MIGA guarantees from potential investors in low-income countries as of that date total 350. While the vast majority of these prospective investments will not proceed for commercial reasons, the sheer number of applications is indicative of the demand for political risk insurance.

MIGA also offers technical and legal assistance to enhance the institutional capacity of host country investment promotion agencies (IPAs). Wherever possible, MIGA seeks to support promotion activities that can be organized on a multicountry or sectoral basis. For example, MIGA has provided extensive support to the promotion of foreign investment in the mining sector in Africa, including the organization of a major mining conference in June 1994 at which 18 Sub-Saharan countries showcased their mining investment opportunities to about 300 prospective investors from North America, Europe, and Asia.

New initiatives for the dissemination of information on investment opportunities in developing countries include a CD-ROM on mining sector investment opportunities in Africa and IPAnet, a global electronic information exchange and communications network on investment opportunities. This network, to be carried over the Internet, will link IPAs, business associations, financial institutions, and other intermediaries involved in the promotion or facilitation of foreign investment.

government institutions responsible for the central role of macroeconomic management, the most important institutions are those responsible for:

- Legal and regulatory systems.
- Public finance, notably the tax and customs administrators that interact closely with the private sector.
- Trade and investment.

No less important are institutions that:

FIGURE 2.1 FOUNDATIONS OF A COMPETITIVE PRIVATE SECTOR

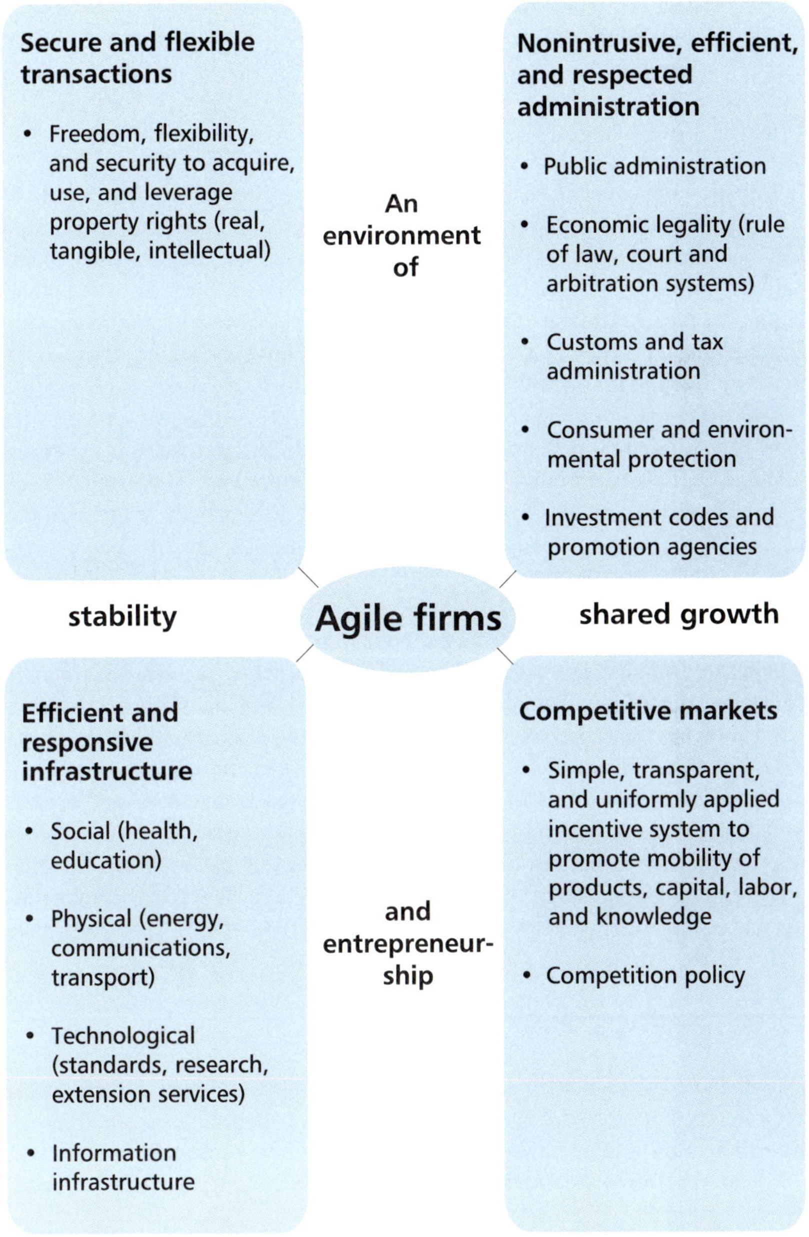

Secure and flexible transactions

- Freedom, flexibility, and security to acquire, use, and leverage property rights (real, tangible, intellectual)

Nonintrusive, efficient, and respected administration

- Public administration

- Economic legality (rule of law, court and arbitration systems)

- Customs and tax administration

- Consumer and environmental protection

- Investment codes and promotion agencies

An environment of

stability   **Agile firms**   shared growth

Efficient and responsive infrastructure

- Social (health, education)

- Physical (energy, communications, transport)

- Technological (standards, research, extension services)

- Information infrastructure

Competitive markets

- Simple, transparent, and uniformly applied incentive system to promote mobility of products, capital, labor, and knowledge

- Competition policy

and entrepreneurship

- Support technological development—universities, standards and metrology agencies, productivity centers, agricultural extension services, and research and development and labor training institutes.
- Facilitate flows of economic, business, market, and technological information.

Building partnerships

In fast-growing countries these institutions have worked closely and regularly with business and labor associations and with other civic groups to address and solve problems that affect the ability of firms to compete internally and externally. Important objectives have also been to change the attitude of the population, the media, and the administration at all levels toward entrepreneurship and legitimate profit-making—and to change the business culture from courting the government for privileges to courting competitive markets for profits.

Governments in some low-income countries have forged partnerships with their private sectors to sharpen the reform agenda and to establish the credibility of the reform program with the business community. The value of such partnerships has been demonstrated in Ghana and Senegal, where private-public consultative mechanisms are helping to bridge the gap between policymakers and the private sector in developing reform programs that enjoy broad support (box 2.3).

An important element of this partnership is the availability of timely and reliable information on economic and business activity. In most low-income countries, this information is incomplete, outdated, and not uniformly accessible—reducing transparency and accountability and increasing the opportunity for corruption. This makes it difficult for governments to formulate and monitor policies. And it limits the ability of entrepreneurs, investors, and lenders to make reasonable judgments about business opportunities and the viability of projects. Government investments in improving the information infrastructure could pay large dividends in increased transparency, greater accountability, and reduced uncertainty—if implemented in collaboration with the private sector through producers associations and chambers of commerce.

Secure, flexible transactions

One of the most important attributes of economies that foster private sector activities is that individuals are free—and believe themselves to be free—to take all actions in their economic interest that are not specifically prohibited.

The legal framework in these market economies has at least four basic economic functions:

- To define the universe of property rights in the system.

- To set a framework for exchanging those rights.
- To set the rules for the entry and exit of actors into and out of productive activities.
- To oversee market structure and behavior in ways that promote competition and protect consumers and the environment.

These four basic functions can be loosely related to well-recognized areas of law. Property rights are defined in the constitution of a country and in more specific laws dealing with tangible and intangible property. These should give individuals the freedom, flexibility, and security to acquire, use,

---

BOX 2.3 OVERCOMING PRIVATE SECTOR SKEPTICISM IN GHANA AND SENEGAL

By the end of the 1980s, Ghana had undertaken major economic reform, yet had achieved little supply response in the private sector. An IDA-sponsored survey of the sector identified regulations inhibiting private sector operations and found that many private entrepreneurs felt that the government was ambivalent toward them.

To address these problems the government formed a private sector advisory group (PSAG), comprising representatives from the private sector and the government, and asked it to develop a set of recommendations for the revision of business regulations. The group's final report was then discussed with private entrepreneurs, and many of its recommendations were adopted, resulting in removal of price controls and business licensing requirements and simplification of foreign direct investment regulations. Equally important, the process reduced the gulf between government and the private sector. Ghana's PSAG has been succeeded by the Business Roundtable, which holds periodic discussions with the government on issues relating to the financial sector, privatization, export promotion, and legal and judicial reforms. These efforts have facilitated privatization and encouraged both domestic and foreign investment.

In Senegal in 1994, the Bank Group sponsored an assessment of the private sector, while the government established a competitiveness review group (CRG) made up of representatives of employer associations, labor unions, and government. The CRG was to look for ways to remove obstacles to economic competitiveness and to involve both government and the private sector in formulating and carrying out economic reform. Supported by technical assistance from IDA, Senegal's CRG has assembled five commissions to poll the private sector view of reforms on important and contentious issues (including *conventions spéciales,* high transaction costs, high taxes, complex government procedures, and lack of competition policy). The commissions' work has resulted in the dismantling of most conventions spéciales and the simplification of business regulations supported by an IDA credit.

and leverage property rights. Exchange is covered generally by contract law. Entry is governed by company and foreign investment law, bankruptcy and exit, by liquidation laws. Finally, to promote competition and protect consumers are antimonopoly and unfair competition laws. These basic areas of law are joined by many other important ones—such as labor, taxation, and banking—in a rich and intricately woven web of laws that constitutes the complex legal framework for private sector activity in advanced market economies.

Important gaps in laws and rules need to be plugged, and the institutional mechanisms for implementing laws and rules need to be strengthened, streamlined, and made more efficient and responsive

---

The challenge in strengthening the legal and judicial system in many low-income countries is twofold: important gaps in laws and rules need to be plugged, and the institutional mechanisms for implementing laws and rules need to be strengthened, streamlined, and made more efficient and responsive. In low-income countries that previously operated under socialist systems, the challenge is to reconstruct the basic elements of the legal and judicial system to create a regime friendly to private property rights.

Four important deficiencies in laws and their implementation are frequently cited:

Laws relating to property rights and collateral. In most low-income countries, legal restrictions or deficiencies in collateral laws limit borrowing options for enterprises, particularly for new and small firms that cannot offer unencumbered landed property. Banks' unwillingness to lend against movable and intangible property stems from the high costs of creating a loan secured by collateral, the slow and costly judicial procedures to repossess and sell collateral, and the inadequate registries for filing claims against collateral—making it difficult for lenders to publicize their security interests.

In Bolivia, the economic cost of deficiencies in collateral laws has reduced equipment investment by as much as $500 million, leading to a loss of potential output of about 2 percent of GDP (box 2.4). In most African countries lending against movable goods (and receivables) is uncommon. In many countries, the problem extends to landed property. Laws for land markets are not clear, land registries have not been updated, and establishing clear unencumbered title to land is difficult. That discourages long-term investment, reduces access to institutional finance, and mutes incentives for the greater productivity and commercialization of agriculture.

BOX 2.4 BOLIVIA: THE ECONOMIC VALUE OF COLLATERAL

In Bolivia commercial bank lending is mainly collateralized by land or the personal guarantee of wealthy individuals. Because of inadequate property laws and legal procedures, assets such as inventory, industrial equipment, and accounts receivable are not considered acceptable collateral. And because the registries for recording security interest in property function poorly, it is hard for lenders to trace claims and identify their collateral in the eyes of the court. Repossessing collateral is made complex and time-consuming by gaps in laws that govern financial transactions. The judicial process for enforcing these laws, for instance, takes considerably longer than the times specified under law. As a consequence of these legal and administrative deficiencies, persons without real estate cannot finance equipment purchases. Only those with unencumbered fixed assets can get credit for working capital. Credit sales are discouraged. Nonbank credit is very expensive. And lenders must rely on criminal rather than civil law to enforce contracts. If deficiencies in laws governing collateral were rectified and financing were easier, demand for equipment in Bolivia could rise by more than $500 million. That in turn would increase the country's output by an estimated $150–$200 million, roughly 2 percent of GDP.

Basic business laws. Many countries have not adapted the business laws introduced by colonial powers to today's economic circumstances. Madagascar's commercial code is virtually unchanged from the French code adopted in 1867. In Sierra Leone, company law dates from 1929 and has undergone few modifications. Business laws need to provide for fuller disclosure that allows outsiders to evaluate the financial position of firms and firms to effectively leverage their assets. One of the biggest problems is inconsistency in laws relating to foreign exchange transactions, income taxes, and customs—a consequence of the failure to repeal obsolete laws and regulations and formulate new laws to reflect changes in policies. For example, despite government policy to provide duty-drawback relief to Nigerian exporters, rules for operation of the scheme have yet to be formulated and incorporated in customs regulations. In most countries, consumer protection laws also are poorly developed, and most countries still lack laws on standards allowing the public or smaller firms to challenge monopolistic behavior.

Laws governing financial transactions. Laws often do not permit full play of financial relationships and instruments. In many African countries, laws and regulations governing capital market transactions are inadequate and an underdeveloped legal framework for leasing prevents small firms from increasing their equipment investments and denies lenders a more secure method of lending to small enterprises. In Ghana, small firms improved their access to credit following introduction of leasing laws.

Most countries have neglected the legal issues of debt recovery. Inefficient adjudication has often rendered court-based remedies ineffective and encouraged willful default. In Bangladesh and India, judicial procedures relating to debt recovery can take years. Extrajudicial foreclosure arrangements—allowing lenders to exercise control rights over the security or operations of firms—are normally not available in most low-income countries. As a result, financial intermediaries prefer to lend only to established firms. Newer and smaller firms without a track record or unencumbered real property find it difficult to get finance.

Sustained growth will require large infusions of capital, much more than entrepreneurs can get from their own resources or from friends and relatives. And expanding access to outside finance—from banks and institutional investors—will require comprehensive revision of laws relating to the creation, trading, and enforcement of security interests.

Laws for arbitration and other dispute resolution mechanisms. In many countries, such laws and mechanisms are not responsive to changing commercial needs. In the absence of quicker alternative dispute resolution mechanisms, firms must rely on tedious court procedures, increasing the costs and risks of market transactions and squelching the opportunities to expand markets.

Specialized institutions, such as law reform commissions, can improve the relevance of laws and provide a mechanism for gradually revising laws on a consensual basis in harmony with existing social and legal traditions. In many low-income countries, these institutions either do not exist or have become moribund, as in Sierra Leone. Strengthening institutional mechanisms for law reform is particularly important for privatization programs, for the private provision of infrastructure services, for attracting foreign investment, and for protecting the interests of small and new enterprises.

Equally important is strengthening public awareness of laws and legal decisions. When the substance and applicability of laws are known only to a few, uncertainty rises for all business decisions. Poor law reporting arrangements, outdated legal indexes, and delayed gazette notifications are the main culprits. In Ghana, there is a considerable backlog of law reporting—and until recently, even summaries of court decisions were unavailable. In Sierra Leone, the last available law reports date back to 1984.

The efficacy of laws depends on disposing of court cases expeditiously. In most low-income countries, adjudication is cumbersome and unreliable. Serving summons, filing suits, obtaining judgments, and executing decrees are all time-consuming. Efficiency is impeded by limited knowledge of economic laws and severe shortages of trained court clerks, process servers, transcribers, and bailiffs. Further handicapping the functioning of the legal and judicial system is the poor state of the physical, logistical, and informational infrastructure. In many low-income countries—such as Bangladesh, Ghana, Sierra Leone, and Tanzania—the facilities for recording court proceedings are rudimentary. Judges often have to record the proceedings manually, so delays in completing cases are common.

In many Sub-Saharan African countries and formerly socialist economies, government agencies are ill-equipped to convert legislative proposals and government intent into coherent legislation. Legislation, rules, regulations, and public notices fail to keep pace with government policy announcements and decisions, particularly in matters relating to investments, foreign exchange, customs, taxes, and finance. That naturally hurts the credibility and timeliness of reforms. The result is confusing and inconsistent legislation that allows civil servants wide latitude in interpretation—thus denying predictability, flexibility, and security for property transactions.

Efforts to improve the quality of legal drafting and analysis can pay large dividends in private investment. Witness the mining sectors in many African countries, where the private sector responded positively to clear, revised mining codes. The Bank Group has been helping low-income countries to address specific deficiencies in laws through technical assistance directed at improving institutional and infrastructure capacity (box 2.5). These efforts are collaborative undertakings by governments, the judiciary, and the private sector, with IDA's support. They are creating a broad consensus about reform and the most effective way of implementing it—to strengthen the legal and regulatory system in low-income countries.

The objective of this effort is to establish, visibly, a rule-based economic system in which the rules governing economic activity are generally available and understood by the population. Those rules are to be enforced uniformly and universally, with a stable, predictable pattern over time. And they are to be changed through transparent means. Such open processes have special merit for countries that have experienced gradual breakdowns in their judicial system—and where the expropriation of private property in the 1960s and 1970s left many private companies, particularly foreign ones, doubtful about the wisdom of continuing to invest.

Competition—and simplified regulation

Competition is fundamental if firms are to court the market for profits and not the state for favors. Regulatory and competition policies have to facilitate market entry and exit, increase factor mobility, offer a level playing field, and reduce transaction costs.

Many low-income countries—especially those in Africa—have made important strides in the past four years in boosting internal and external

BOX 2.5 LEGAL REFORM: A NEW AND GROWING BUSINESS

Member countries have increasingly sought IDA assistance to improve their legal systems. IDA adjustment credits have supported programs that included amending specific laws related to economic efficiency.

■ Under a structural adjustment credit in Benin, specific legal measures were introduced to enhance loan recoveries—including reform of relevant judicial procedures, land title records, and commercial laws.

■ Bolivia's structural adjustment credit supported both the enactment and enforcement of new banking laws and regulations.

Investment credits and technical assistance credits have helped countries examine legal issues hindering the development of a specific sector.

■ In Kenya, the Parastatal Reform and Privatization Project financed a comprehensive review of laws affecting the development of the private sector and the restructuring of public enterprises.

■ Côte d'Ivoire's Economic Management Project enabled the Ministry of Justice to strengthen laws and judicial procedures related to commerce.

■ Mozambique's Roads and Coastal Shipping Project provided assistance for the revision of laws and regulations for small ports and coastal shipping.

In recent years, it has become increasingly clear that—to improve a country's ability to enact, apply, and enforce laws—legal reform needs to be comprehensive. Free-standing technical assistance credits and grant funds have been used to address major reform issues in the legal and judicial sector.

■ Under the Zambia Financial and Legal Management Project, a comprehensive training program for legal and paralegal staff is being carried out within both the judiciary and government, and support is being provided for upgrading the physical infrastructure and logistic capabilities.

■ In Tanzania, a Financial and Legal Management Upgrading Project is assisting the government to undertake a review of commercial laws, upgrade the attorney general's office and court libraries, undertake various legal studies, and train judges, magistrates, and administrative officers of the courts.

■ In China, a free-standing legal technical assistance project is supporting legislative subprojects, legal training subprojects, and institutional support for core legal agencies.

■ In Viet Nam, IDA is providing assistance in the drafting of laws governing state enterprises, bankruptcy, and land ownership.

To improve the efficiency of land markets, IDA has assisted low-income countries in rationalizing land laws, in harmonizing them with customary laws, in undertaking land surveys and in strengthening land titling, adjudication, and registration procedures. This support includes, for example, improvements in the system of recording various types of land rights in Côte d'Ivoire, in mapping and land conveyancing procedures and adjudication of land disputes in Ghana, and in land titling procedures in Albania.

competition. But most governments are still reluctant to relinquish discretionary latitude in their regulatory powers. They remain concerned about monopoly profits, the misuse of incentives, and the vulnerability of small, indigenous entrepreneurs. Some of these concerns are justified, insofar as they relate to unfair trade practices. But the evidence suggests that in many instances special incentives get misused. Small firms fail to benefit while larger, well-connected firms and public firms get around the regulations, circumventing the competition that the rules were supposed to achieve.

The challenge for government is to create incentives for firms to invest and compete for a larger market and to provide the means to do so

Experience from developing and industrial countries alike suggests there are simpler, cheaper, and more effective ways to address these concerns. A competitive trade regime with low uniform rates of effective protection can deter monopolistic behavior. Low and uniform rates of taxation can minimize the misuse of fiscal and tax incentives. Better laws and better-functioning legal institutions can offer transparent and equitable methods of protection without distorting incentives. Firms are more likely to grow and remain competitive when trade expands, when investments can be made easily, and when regulations are simple and transparent.

The challenge for government is to create incentives for firms to invest and compete for a larger market and to provide the means to do so. Doing this implies reducing barriers to trade, encouraging domestic and foreign investment, and applying simple regulations openly and expeditiously, supported by efficient infrastructure. Many countries have made progress in reducing trade barriers. The challenge now is to reduce quickly and systematically the burden and cost of business regulation and poorly performing infrastructure while maintaining steady progress on dismantling trade barriers.

Promote external and internal competition

Most countries, often with the help of IDA, have made notable progress in reforming their exchange rates and trade regimes, with reforming African economies notable among them (box 2.6). Exchange rate reforms have eliminated large black market premiums in countries where the official exchange rate had been kept artificially low. Devaluations, leading to large real exchange rate depreciations, and reduced rationing of foreign exchange, often through auctions, have been among the biggest changes. Similarly, these countries removed most

BOX 2.6 IDA SUPPORT FOR AN ATTRACTIVE BUSINESS ENVIRONMENT

IDA has worked closely with governments in low-income countries to establish an attractive business environment for the private sector. It has provided extensive financial and technical support for policy interventions that reduce distortions in the economy, remove barriers to international and domestic competition, and minimize regulatory burdens on the private sector. The nature of IDA's support has evolved over the past decade. In the 1980s, as part of macroeconomic stabilization programs, IDA supported reforms relating to foreign exchange and trade regimes. Since then, most countries in Africa have substantially eliminated black market premiums (particularly Ghana, Uganda, Mozambique, and Zimbabwe) and reduced exchange controls. IDA also supported trade reforms that reduced tariffs (for example, in Bangladesh, Ghana, and India), eliminated quantitative restrictions (for example, in Burundi, Ghana, Senegal, and Zambia), and replaced quantitative restrictions with tariffs (for example, in Burundi, Ghana, Madagascar, and Zambia). Trade reforms aimed at further reductions in tariff and nontariff barriers continue to receive attention in IDA operations.

Since the end of the 1980s, the focus of IDA support has shifted toward structural and sectoral reforms. These include:
- Eliminating or reducing the number of products subject to price controls (as in the Central African Republic, Madagascar, Niger, Sierra Leone, Tanzania, and Uganda).
- Eliminating controls on profit margins (as in Gabon, Guinea-Bissau, and Madagascar).
- Ending parastatal monopolies in production, distribution and marketing (as in Ethiopia, Ghana, and Tanzania).
- Abolishing or easing product and sector licensing policies (as in Côte d'Ivoire, Ghana, India, and Senegal).
- Eliminating punitive rates of taxation, replacing turnover taxes with value-added taxes, and simplifying tax structures, administration, and

quantitative restrictions and foreign exchange licensing. But most governments in Africa have adopted a gradual approach to reducing tariffs—both because of the importance of trade taxes for revenues and because of the perceived need to phase in reductions in effective protection. Progress has focused on simplifying and reducing maximum tariff rates (table 2.2). Similarly, tariff collection has improved, though in some countries average tariff collection rates remain below average statutory tariffs, largely because of discretionary exemptions.

Except in Sri Lanka, average tariffs in South Asia are still high and more dispersed relative to other regions, thereby holding back exports and muting competition in domestic markets. Quantitative restrictions still afford considerable protection to a wide range of products, particularly consumer goods. Some countries, such as Bangladesh, India, and Pakistan, have only recently accelerated their tariff reforms. China has taken steps to reduce tariffs and has

BOX 2.6 (continued)

compliance (as in Bangladesh, Ghana, India, and Uganda).

■ Revising and streamlining investment codes (as in Benin, Ghana, Guinea-Bissau, Mauritania, and Uganda).

■ Simplifying regulations governing enterprise creation and operation (as in Burundi, Central African Republic, and Ghana).

■ Enacting new labor legislation (as in Burkina Faso and Gabon).

■ Reducing restrictions on hiring and discharging labor (as in Benin, Burundi, Lao People's Democratic Republic, and Zimbabwe).

■ Establishing safety nets for retrenched labor (as in Bangladesh, Cape Verde, and India).

Between fiscal years 1988 and 1994, IDA's average annual lending in support of favorable yet competitive business environments was $1.6 billion—about 28 percent of IDA average annual lending. The number of projects with explicit reform components averaged 29 each year. Reforms have been supported through a wide range of sectors and lending instruments. In Africa, structural and sector adjustment operations have been used as effective and comprehensive instruments for improving the business environment. Between 1988 and 1994, trade reforms were supported in 18 adjustment operations, price reforms in 39, reforms in regulations and regulatory institutions relating to customs, taxes, and investments in 37, reform of sector-specific investment policies in 22, and reforms of labor markets in 23. In addition, sector-specific investment operations in agriculture, infrastructure, mining, energy, and industrial sectors have been used in all IDA-eligible low-income countries to address specific impediments to private investment. Finally, through a significant program of economic and sector work, IDA has worked closely with governments and the private sector to identify critical constraints and institutional deficiencies in the incentive and regulatory framework.

indicated its intention to phase out most quota restrictions. It also intends to unify its large domestic market by building up over the next three years with IDA assistance a comprehensive system of economic trade laws and regulations that apply uniformly across the country.

The major impact of liberalizing trade has been to give firms easier access to technology, capital, and intermediate goods and critical raw materials. Tariff reform increases internal competition, reduces production costs, improves product range and quality, and increases the incentive to export. In India, the reduction in inventory costs alone probably amounts to several percentage points of total cost. Recent surveys in Africa also show that industry and services have gained because of increased access to production inputs, with important gains for informal sector activities and the smaller businesses in the formal sector. In the reforming economies of Sub-Saharan Africa, industry

TABLE 2.2 TARIFF RATES IN SELECTED LOW-INCOME COUNTRIES

Country	Average unweighted tariff rates (percent)	Quantitative restrictions (QRs)
China (1992)	43	Up to 50% of imports covered by QRs
Viet Nam (1991)	11	Nearly all QRs were replaced by tariffs in 1994
Bangladesh (1994)	30	Less than 10% of tariff lines are covered by QRs
India (1994)	53	38% of tariff lines are covered by QRs
Pakistan (1994)	50	The negative list has been reduced from 215 categories to 75, and the restricted list has been removed
Sri Lanka (1994)	25	All QRs have been removed
Cameroon (1994)	16	All QRs have been removed
Côte d'Ivoire (1994)	19	Up to 50% of QRs were removed in 1994, and 90% of nonoil imports will be free by January 1996
Ghana (1991)	17	All QRs have been removed
Kenya (1994)	26	No significant QRs
Nigeria (1990)	33	20% of industrial production and 30% of agricultural production were covered by QRs in 1994
Senegal (1994)	a	QRs eliminated, except for items agreed with specific firms prior to 1987. These will be replaced by a 20% import surcharge
Tanzania (1992)	33	QRs to be eliminated as part of the reform program
Zambia (1994)	25	No significant QRs

a. Tariff rates range between 10 percent and 45 percent. Luxury items are subject to an additional 20 percent import duty.
Source: World Bank data.

grew by 4.3 percent a year during 1987–93 after falling by 3.0 percent a year during 1981–86. Similar accelerations in growth and exports were found in services and agriculture between the two periods as firms, particularly smaller firms, successfully adapted to new incentives by changing the product mix, inventory, and labor costs under their control. New labor-intensive and export-oriented businesses also emerged in agriculture and services in response to the altered incentive structure. And evidence from several African countries suggests that these firms tend to be more robust than their predecessors—more oriented to global markets and with better-educated entrepreneurs.

One of the best ways to acquire technology and increase the capacity to respond and compete is through trade. Imports of capital goods, equipment,

and inputs embody years of acquired knowledge. The technical support services that generally accompany these imports are also a major source of know-
how for improving production capabilities. So are buyers of a country's
manufactured exports. Then, through domestic trade and labor mobility, this
know-how gets widely diffused throughout the economy.

The importance of trade in acquiring technology through imports of capital goods, equipment, and inputs is demonstrated by the growth of export-oriented garment industries in Bangladesh, cut flowers in Colombia and Kenya,
and diamond cutting in India, as well as by the high growth in the coastal
regions of China, where tariff barriers were almost totally eliminated.

Further reform efforts have been slowed because of concerns expressed
by governments and the private sector that rapid liberalization will lead to deindustrialization, decimate small and medium-size industries, and retard the
growth of nascent domestic entrepreneurship. True, firms suffer when incentives change, especially capital-intensive public enterprises that have
developed behind tariff barriers or under the umbrella of public protection and
whose domestic market may shrink as they face import competition. But this
is seldom the case in low-income countries. Exemptions and quantitative
restrictions abound, particularly in Asia. And tariffs remain high—it is not
uncommon to find effective rates of protection between 40 and 60 percent. This
distorts the markets, mutes competition, and inhibits exports.

In many countries, however, a good part of effective protection is eroded by
the high cost of doing business stemming from inefficient public enterprises and
utilities, onerous regulatory requirements, poor quality and high cost of supply
from public sector, and heavy financing costs. Increasing tariff and nontariff protection is self-defeating because it limits the firms' ability to obtain the inputs
necessary to compete both internally and externally. Similarly, selective and temporary protection, as applied in East Asia, requires a capable and honest civil service that can administer, monitor, and adapt these incentives quickly to market
conditions. In most low-income countries, there is little domestic competition,
and civil services are weak. So, the emphasis has to be on the systematic reduction of the heavy costs of excessive economic and administrative regulation, one
of the root causes of the problem. This reduction complements the continuing
efforts to lower effective rates of protection, reduce tariff dispersion, eliminate
quantitative restrictions, and remove impediments to internal trade. The following sections deal with various aspects of the regulatory environment.

Eliminate preferential treatment of the public sector

A major obstacle to making markets competitive is the dominance of state-
owned enterprises in key sectors of the economy (see chapter 1). In many countries, the high cost and poor quality of inputs provided by state-owned

enterprises (utilities and others) increase production cost by as much as 30 percent and deprive firms of opportunities both inside and outside the country. In Africa, state monopolies for agricultural commodity exports have held back growth of the private sector.

Costly monopoly marketing arrangements involving state-owned marketing enterprises have reduced returns to farmers and muted the impact of trade and exchange rate reforms intended to improve incentives for farmers. A desire to tap an easy source of revenue to feed hungry government coffers has been one of the main reasons for continuing to control commodity exports. Even where state marketing boards have been abolished, de facto monopolies still thrive. Private entry has been restricted through licensing arrangements, transport restrictions, and control over processing and storage facilities. And in many instances, state marketing boards enjoy privileged access to financing from state-owned commercial banks.

One argument for government intervention in agricultural markets is to prevent the exploitation of farmers and consumers by marketing middlemen. Yet in many instances the entry of private traders has had a positive impact (box 2.7). Traders provide credit and technical advice to farmers. And by

---

BOX 2.7 THE AGRICULTURE SECTOR RESPONDS TO MARKET REFORMS

Tanzania. In 1990, all restrictions on private grain purchases were removed at the farm level. And despite many remaining legal, regulatory, and infrastructure obstacles, private traders have managed to improve farmers' access to markets, increase food supplies, and stabilize food prices in urban areas. Free entry has also increased competition, reduced profit margins in private trading, and contributed to the revival of the cashew nut sector. With farmers now having their crops collected early and being paid promptly, production went from 29,000 tons in 1990–91 to 41,000 tons in 1992–93. Cashew farmers are beginning to rehabilitate their farms and plant new trees.

Malawi. Following a series of reforms, private participation in domestic maize marketing has increased con-siderably. Despite unfair competition from the state-owned marketing agency, private producers have managed to capture a considerable share of the domestic market by paying farmers substantially higher prices than the state-owned agency.

India. A host of regulations prevented domestic private companies from participating in the seed industry until the early 1980s, when these polices were liberalized. By 1990, the private sector's share in the value of commercial seed sales reached roughly 70 percent, with growth being most rapid in sorghum, pearl millet, cotton, and vegetables. Older companies spun off numerous new companies, considerably increasing competition and offering farmers greater choice in their seed purchases.

investing in vehicles and collection points for moving inputs and outputs, traders strengthen rural infrastructure and connect farmers to bigger markets.

By simplifying regulations for private entry and privatizing financial systems to expand access to credit beyond government agencies and a handful of privileged traders, governments can foster considerable competition in rural marketing. And by increasing public investments in rural infrastructure such as roads and market facilities, governments can reduce entry costs and spur competition.

Simplify regulations to reduce the cost of doing business

One of the biggest complaints of firms in low-income countries relates to the complex maze of opaque, restrictive, and highly discretionary regulations for investments, business operations, fiscal incentives, customs, and taxes. These regulations thwart competition, segment markets, increase the cost of doing business, and discourage foreign direct investment. They have encouraged rent-seeking strategies where larger profits can be made by manipulating rules and excluding competition than by improving competitive capabilities.

Many countries have undertaken systematic efforts to reduce the burden of excessive regulation. When these reform efforts are viewed as credible, firms react positively, as in India (box 2.8). The challenge for governments is to reduce trade and investment impediments, reduce barriers to entry and exit, increase labor mobility, simplify regulatory tax administration, and implement regulations through responsive and accountable public institutions.

Even many countries that have simplified investment licensing still have discretionary business licensing to grant special privileges and monopolies to some firms at considerable cost to the rest of the economy. In India, layers of federal and state policies continue to inhibit interstate commerce, depriving entrepreneurs from economies of scale and scope. Product reservation, licensing, and industrial location policies have segmented markets, increased prices for consumers, and removed incentives for efficiency and productivity improvements. As a result, it is not unusual to see inefficient firms operating at a fraction of installed capacity for extended periods, while maintaining the same market share as efficient firms.

In Senegal, favored firms received such special long-term concessions as tax incentives, production and distribution monopolies, import protection, and price guarantees. A domestic sugar monopoly has cost the economy some $55 million a year, $7 million of it in direct subsidies. This arrangement has also prevented another local firm from selling sugar cubes in the domestic market at half the monopoly's price. Having imposed considerable costs on the rest of the economy—and reduced competition—these concessions are now being progressively removed.

BOX 2.8 INDIA: CREDIBLE REFORMS LEAD TO STRONG SUPPLY RESPONSE

Since 1991, India has been implementing economic reforms that have been moving its private sector to the lead in its development strategy. Investment deregulation, trade liberalization, financial reforms, and tax reforms have transformed the environment for private investment. The government has deregulated and opened most areas of the economy to the private sector, reduced tariffs and quantitative restrictions, and opened the financial sector to private competition.

■ In manufacturing, licensing requirements now apply to only 15 listed industries.

■ In mining, 13 minerals previously reserved for the public sector are now open to the private sector.

■ In some areas of infrastructure, private participation is now possible and encouraged—in the power sector private entry is unrestricted, with up to 100 percent foreign ownership. Private airlines compete with the state airline on domestic routes. The private sector can enter the railways sector through "own your wagon" schemes.

Coastal shipping has been completely deregulated.

Even in sectors that are still reserved for the public sector, such as telecommunications, petroleum, coal, and postal services, the government has taken a liberal stance toward private investments. Private operators can provide value-added services in telecommunications. Private courier services can compete with government postal services. And more private investment is being sought in the petroleum sector.

Maximum tariffs have been slashed from 400 percent in 1990–91 to 65 percent in 1994–95. Average tariffs have declined from 128 percent in 1990–91 to 53 percent in 1994–95. Import licensing for capital and intermediate goods has been eliminated, and customs duties have been rationalized to lower capital and input costs. Export controls on agricultural commodities have also been reduced.

In the financial sector, interest rates have been partially liberalized. International standards on prudential

When fiscal incentives are provided case-by-case, protracted negotiations with government agencies are common. Firms lacking political clout are usually blocked out. In the Philippines, the Board of Investments approves tax and duty exemptions on imported capital equipment and on investments in "pioneer" sectors for individual companies. Large firms oriented toward domestic markets enjoy most of the benefits—to the exclusion of small and medium-size firms that are important for exports.

There is growing acceptance of the principle that licensing should serve to register and monitor enterprises and not to restrict entry. The existence of productive capacity is no longer a criterion for denying new licenses in Ghana. The licensing of new industries has recently been simplified or removed from

BOX 2.8 (continued)

lending norms and capital adequacy guidelines have been adopted. Government financial institutions have been encouraged to raise equity. And private entry in the banking system has been allowed. The government is also considering new private entry in the insurance sector.

Laws and regulations for foreign investment have been made more flexible and less discretionary. Automatic approval for 51 percent foreign equity participation is allowed in 34 "high priority" industries. New rules for foreign portfolio investments have been instituted to attract foreign capital in the stock markets.

A comprehensive program of tax reforms is being implemented. Corporate income taxes have been reduced. The excise system is being simplified and converted into a value-added tax system with fewer different rates. Invoices are used for the determination of value.

Reforms at the federal level are being accompanied by state initiatives to simplify investment and business regulations. In Gujarat, private participation has been allowed in the development of ports and in power generation. In Kerala, a green-channel scheme has been introduced to expedite industrial clearance. In Uttar Pradesh, inspections by various government agencies are being simplified. And in Andhra Pradesh and Orissa, power purchase agreements with private suppliers have been signed.

Results have been significant. Foreign direct investment rose from $165 million in 1990 to more than $600 million in 1993–94. Portfolio investment went from nearly nothing in 1991–92 to more than $4 billion in 1993–94. Exports grew by 20 percent in 1993–94. Private air operators have captured 40 percent of domestic air traffic business and spurred the state airline to improve its customer services. Some 87 independent power project proposals (total capacity of about 50,000 megawatts) have been submitted. Ten new private banks have received banking licenses, and eight new foreign banks have established branch operations.

ministerial discretion in Zambia and Zimbabwe. Some countries have tried to streamline investment applications through "one-stop shops," which have had mixed results. In Mali and Senegal, the Guichet Unique undertakes regulatory and fiscal formalities for applicants, but entrepreneurs complain that they have to provide excessive documentation and must often still pursue approvals from various ministries.

The costs of all this for doing business are clear and documented. Business licenses cost formal Kenyan firms an estimated 5 percent of sales. And Bolivian enterprises have to complete as many as 86 registers and records, a time-consuming process that can reduce before-tax profit of 25 percent to as little as 5 percent.

Solving these problems begins at the top—with a conviction that reducing the interference and hostility to business at the working level is a top priority. Part of the problem in many countries is that the commitment to liberalization at the highest levels of government has not yet reached the middle and lower levels of government, where hostility and corruption are often compounded by poorly trained civil servants. Beyond that are technical issues of streamlining regulations and their administration and aggressively promoting investment opportunities.

Promote labor mobility

Labor reform is another area of increasing concern, particularly in large organized sectors. Though detailed information on labor markets is not available for many low-income countries, government regulation generally reduces labor mobility. Large firms bear the brunt of rigid labor laws that constrain them from restructuring their operations, force smaller capacity expansions than otherwise, and reduce employment creation by encouraging capital-intensive modes of production.

Rigid labor laws have also slowed the pace of economic reforms, privatization, and state enterprise reforms. In India, where the organized industrial sector accounts for 80 percent of industrial value added, constraints on rationalizing the labor force are a heavy drag on industrial growth. In China, the competitiveness of the state-owned sector has been crimped by the need to maintain high employment and provide workers with housing, medical care, schools, transport, and other social services not usually provided by other firms. Their labor costs are more than twice those of collectively-owned enterprises.

The challenge is to unbundle these services and transfer them to municipalities or commercial entities so that firms can operate on a commercial basis and labor is free to seek opportunities elsewhere.

Simplify customs and tax structures and administration

Customs and tax institutions also take a heavy toll. Fully one-third of the time required to ship freight between landlocked Mali and neighboring ports in Lomé and Abidjan is for customs clearances. Few Sub-Saharan countries have an effective system of rebating domestic taxes on exports. Duty drawback and bonded warehouse systems are not well developed or widely publicized. Firms have to engage in extensive negotiations to take advantage of export programs, incurring delays and reduced competitiveness in the process.

In many countries, tax agencies have considerable latitude in the content and timing of their decisions. In Egypt, a business may not know its tax liability for ten years after submitting its declaration. Cumbersome sales tax and excise duty procedures hinder the operations of firms and encourage tax evasion in many countries. Bangladesh and India are gradually replacing these taxes with a value-added tax (VAT) and simplifying tax administration while maintaining the buoyancy of revenues. Ghana is also considering a VAT to replace its sales tax. To overhaul a complex and fragmented tax system, and to overcome deficiencies that inject considerable uncertainty into business operations, China has initiated a tax reform program covering tax structure, tax administration, and revenue sharing between the center and the provinces.

Promote foreign direct investment

In most low-income countries, the small enterprise sector has the greatest need for technology and market access—and could benefit most from a larger presence by foreign firms. FDI plays a powerful role in stimulating competition and the growth of the domestic private sector. In addition to providing capital, foreign firms transfer technologies and management skills and give domestic firms access to export markets. Domestic and foreign trading companies have been particularly important in international product and information markets and have provided logistical and trade financing support that has been especially valuable to smaller firms.

In 1993, worldwide FDI flows were $200 billion, with the developing country share around $65 billion. Most of this FDI was concentrated in Latin America, East Asia, and China, though there was a significant increase in India and Pakistan. Sub-Saharan Africa had only limited success, attracting only $700 million in 1993, mainly in petroleum and mining where special efforts had been made to attract foreign investment (box 2.9). In other sectors Sub-Saharan countries experienced disinvestment and exodus by foreign firms due to the uncertain political and economic conditions and the high cost of doing business. A recent study indicates that over the past decade or so more than half the British companies that had investments in Sub-Saharan Africa have subsequently disinvested from the area (Bennell 1995). Similar trends appear to be prevalent among firms from other countries, particularly France, Germany, and the United States.

Special efforts of the type initiated for mining and oil sectors may be necessary for reversing the exodus of foreign firms and for stimulating new foreign investment in the manufacturing and service sectors. The powerful impact of FDI on the domestic private sector and exports is vividly demonstrated by the garments industry in Bangladesh, where links between Korean firms created a new class of local entrepreneurs and are helping Bangladesh reduce its dependence on jute exports (box 2.10). In Africa too, foreign investors could play a vital role in overcoming problems of small domestic markets and weak global linkages.

BOX 2.9 PROMOTING FDI IN THE PETROLEUM SECTOR

Starting in the late 1970s the World Bank undertook a series of 45 petroleum exploration promotion projects, of which 20 were in IDA-eligible countries—mainly in Africa. The objective was to attract the private sector into oil and gas exploration and production. The government's role changed from that of primary risk-taker to that of policymaker and regulator, with the private sector taking the exploration and subsequent production risk. These projects provided assistance to low-income countries in:

■ Assessing their national oil and gas resource endowment.

■ Establishing a modern technical data repository.

■ Developing a promotion strategy based on a modern petroleum law, standard oil contracts, fair taxation legislation, and access to the government's technical database.

■ Negotiating contracts with international oil companies.

■ Developing a contract compliance and regulatory agency.

These promotions were successful in obtaining about $500 million in investment by the international oil industry. And they made the private sector the financial risk-taker while strengthening the government's role as policymaker and regulator. The same approach holds promise for promoting private participation in infrastructure, which involves many similar elements.

In addition to improving their business environments, low-income countries can benefit from active promotion efforts and marketing their countries aggressively, particularly to attract employment-generating and skills-enhancing joint ventures. Doing this will take changes in FDI laws and approval processes (single windows for private investment). Also important are simplified procedures for employing foreign experts, assurances for transfers of profits and capital, and less discrimination between foreign firms and the domestic business sector. In this context,the Foreign Investment Advisory Service (FIAS) has been assisting low-income countries to develop more effective investment regimes, often in conjunction with IDA (box 2.11). Countries can also benefit from taking part in international conventions, institutions, and forums that govern trade and investment and provide predictable and credible systems for dispute resolution and settlement.

Promote regional integration

Bureaucratic restrictions and uncoordinated policies inhibit the free movement of goods, capital, and people between countries in Sub-Saharan Africa. The result: limited official foreign trade, considerable smuggling, and small markets. In recognition of the need to promote freer movement of goods, capital,

BOX 2.10 THE CATALYTIC ROLE OF FDI IN BANGLADESH

Despite low wages and the absence of import quotas during the late 1970s, Bangladesh's garment export industry failed to emerge because it lacked both production technology and access to world markets. Then Noorul Quader, a retired government official who had started the Desh Garment Company, signed a collaboration agreement with Korea's Daewoo. Daewoo was to train Desh workers, identify and install machinery, start up production, and market Desh's output. Daewoo and Desh Garments also worked with government officials to establish, for the first time in Bangladesh, official free-trade status for garment factories that were entirely export-oriented. And the government instituted a special bonded warehouse scheme.

This collaboration enabled Desh to enter foreign markets, and between fiscal 1980 and 1987 garment exports went from $55,000 to $5.2 million.

Observing the success of Desh Garments, Desh employees went on to establish their own garment assembly units.

The success of the collaboration encouraged other Korean garment exporters to use Bangladesh as an export platform and take advantage of the favorable treatment accorded to Bangladesh under the Multi-Fibre Agreement. Private investment in the garment sector and production and marketing know-how increased rapidly. The number of garment assembly units increased from 21 in 1983 to 1,630 in 1993, and garment exports skyrocketed to $1.2 billion in 1992–93, when they accounted for 52 percent of Bangladesh's total exports. The creation of an entirely new export industry enabled Bangladesh to reduce its reliance on jute exports and provided gainful employment to a large number of semiskilled female workers.

and people, many countries are starting to coordinate and harmonize tariffs, border controls, payments arrangements, taxation, investments, and business regulations. Currently, three such initiatives exist: first, economic integration arrangements between countries in Eastern and Southern Africa and the Indian Ocean; second, the Union Monétaire Ouest Africaine (UMOA), designed to convert the monetary union among seven West African countries into a full economic union; and third, the Union Douanière des Etats de L'Afrique Centrale (UDEAC), designed to facilitate cross-border movement of goods in six Central African countries.

The major benefits will come from removing restrictions that impede flows of people, capital, and goods—and that segment geographically contiguous markets. In addition, there is considerable untapped potential for regional cooperation in power, transportation, and distribution (particularly petroleum products), which would reduce the costs of doing business. Also providing a strong impetus for regional integration, as in other parts of the world, is the development of regional growth poles—such as South Africa and

BOX 2.11 FIAS PAVES THE WAY FOR FOREIGN DIRECT INVESTMENT

The Foreign Investment Advisory Service (FIAS) helps developing countries shape policies and institutions conducive to foreign direct investment. FIAS advises governments about policies and regulations, relationships with foreign investors, and institutional strengthening. It promotes openness, ease of establishment, transparency in decisionmaking, and no discrimination between foreign and domestic investors. Advice on institutional arrangements emphasizes investment promotion, objective criteria for approvals, and reducing the complexity of approval procedures. To strengthen institutions, governments are advised to specify the characteristics of investment promotion agencies, define their relationships with government ministries and institutions, specify their organizational structure, and identify their training needs.

Between 1991 and 1993, FIAS provided policy and institutional advice to 29 low-income countries. Particularly in Africa, this advice often was part of IDA-sponsored structural adjustment programs. Combining FIAS's expertise with the implementation mechanisms of IDA credits has speeded the pace of policy and institutional reform. Now, low-income countries are increasingly seeking FIAS advice on their own.

In fostering investor-friendly environments, FIAS's impact has been significant. In Asia, nearly every country has followed at least part of the FIAS recommendations. In Bangladesh, FIAS suggestions led to an improvement of the legal framework regulating foreign and domestic private investors and a Board of Investment was set up to promote investment. In Viet Nam, FIAS helped the government adopt a new investment law.

In Africa, FIAS has worked in 26 countries since 1986, of which 18 are IDA-eligible countries.

■ Based on an FIAS diagnostic review, Burkina Faso's government abolished most price controls and relaxed trade regulations.

■ In Ghana, FIAS helped develop a new and more liberal investment code, which has now been adopted and helped the Ghana Investment Promotion Center develop a new organizational plan and investment promotion program.

■ In Guinea Bissau, FIAS helped devise a liberalized investment regime.

■ As part of an IDA structural credit in Mauritania, FIAS recommended new laws regarding investments, foreign exchange allocation to investors, and investment approvals, which are now being implemented.

■ Under another IDA credit, Lesotho has adopted FIAS recommendations relating to an investment promotion agency and strategy.

Between 1991 and 1993 FIAS also achieved considerable success in institutional development. FIAS helped seven low-income countries establish investment organizations, four devoted exclusively to investment promotion. And FIAS helped four countries restructure investment bodies to emphasize investment promotion.

Zimbabwe in the south, Côte d'Ivoire, Ghana, and Nigeria in the west, and Kenya, Tanzania, and Uganda in the east. They could have an important pull effect on growth throughout Africa if the impediments to local and foreign investors and to movements of goods, people, and capital are removed. They could also help promote FDI through enlarging markets. Such regional cooperation and integration should be seen not as a substitute for opening up to the global economy, but as a way of assisting firms to connect to global markets at lower cost.

Enterprise development

In Africa and the smaller low-income countries, the larger firms are either public enterprises or foreign firms. Most indigenous entrepreneurs operate microenterprises in the informal sector, mainly in services in urban and rural areas.

The population of medium-size firms is small—hence the term "missing middle"—firms that elsewhere have been most dynamic in generating employment and increasing wages.

Informal sector

Information on the size of the informal sector is often difficult to obtain. But surveys suggest that in most low-income countries informal sector firms play a significant role, employing as much as 60 percent of the urban labor force. In Burkina Faso, the informal sector accounted for 32 percent of GDP according to the official 1985 census; in Chad, it accounts for 75 percent of employment in the capital city of N' Djamena; in Guinea, about 62 percent of GDP; and in South Africa, about 30–50 percent of the work force.

The informal sector performs vital functions—both for equity and growth. By providing employment and means of income stabilization, the sector acts as a safety valve, especially during difficult economic times. It helps stem rural to urban migration and absorbs social pressures generated by such migration. Largely relying on women, the sector enhances their economic and social status. Most important, the informal sector is the seedbed for entrepreneurial development—in many countries, up to 50 percent of all small firms started out in the informal sector. Characterized by high rates of exit and entry, it is the most dynamic sector. This churning-up process, besides being a constant source of new employment, makes it possible for at least a few entrepreneurs to move up the business ladder.

Firms in the informal sector benefit from economic liberalization, which gives them easier access to inputs at more reasonable prices. But the sector still faces constraints. In many countries, the high cost of complying with regulations often inhibits growth of informal firms and slows their transition into the formal sector—and the attendant benefits of better technology, bigger markets, and greater economies of scale. It also condemns them to low-productivity activities and prevents labor from being utilized more productively. Removing the burdensome regulations identified in the preceding sections will help make the fullest use of the economic functions performed by firms in the informal sector. And giving those firms better access to water, roads, power, and telecommunications will also help raise their productivity and earnings.

The growth of the informal sector is also constrained by limited access to finance. Traditional financial institutions and directed credit programs run by governments have been largely unsuccessful in servicing the needs of this sector. But in many countries—such as Bangladesh, Bolivia, Kenya, and South Africa—community-based institutions have managed to provide a broad range of financial services and technical assistance, as discussed in chapter 4.

Small and medium-size enterprises

The technological and organizational revolution now under way in the global economy is not driven by large, capital-intensive industrial firms. It is driven instead by small and medium-size enterprises (SMEs)—labor intensive in nature, with quick start-up times and agile responses to rapidly shifting markets and technologies. Typically, SMEs are the firms that create the greatest employment opportunities at increasing wages. But they face constraints (box 2.12), so governments often have special programs of subsidies, tax exemptions, and product reservations to support them. These programs have done less to promote a competitive private sector than have policies emphasizing growth—supplemented by programs that address the specific needs of small enterprises for production technology, for easier access to markets, and for credit, management, and labor training services.

Consider India's experience. Small enterprises there operate under product reservation policies that restrict competition from larger firms. Small firms enjoy tax concessions and access to credit on concessional terms from the banking system. These protectionist policies have increased the number of small firms, but reduced their productivity and competitiveness. A significant number of these firms are sick and in need of modernization.

Beyond policy reforms

By contrast, governments in Indonesia, Korea, Taiwan (China), and Thailand have made special efforts to remove impediments to trade and investment and eased the regulatory burdens on SMEs. Freed from these constraints, SMEs have benefited from subcontracting activities with larger firms and

BOX 2.12 THE HARD LIFE OF SMALL AND MEDIUM-SIZE ENTERPRISES

Throughout the developing world, small and medium-size enterprises (SMEs) are condemned to a cycle of low productivity, stunted growth, and unstable incomes. Here are the reasons:

Restricted access to institutional financial services. Companies that lack collateral are frequently denied access to necessary financing. While financial intermediaries are often reluctant to lend to SMEs for sound financial reasons (such as the high transaction cost of monitoring), badly functioning financial systems, ineffective laws on collateral, and poor enforcement of financial contracts also limit access to credit.

Lack of access to markets. SMEs' failure to find markets for their products and services often results from inadequate physical infrastructure, high transport costs, and inadequate information about markets.

Lack of access to inputs. Difficulty in getting physical inputs largely stems from input markets that function badly—including those controlled by large parastatals that have preferential access to inputs.

Inadequate technical skills. Unlike large enterprises, SMEs lack the financial and time resources needed to train workers—who often have little formal education. They also have neither the resources to obtain appropriate technology, nor sufficient access to information on it. The combination of rudimentary technology and poor skills makes for low-quality, uncompetitive products.

Restrictive policies and regulations. While SMEs generally regard policy and regulation as less problematic than credit or physical inputs, excessive bureaucratic procedures and the lack of clear-cut regulatory norms impose high transaction costs that deter them from expanding. Indeed, it is often argued that the scarcity of medium-size enterprises in Africa is largely the result of a highly restrictive regulatory environment.

Distorted incentives for growth. Special support programs to promote SME growth distort the overall incentive system and are thus more harmful than beneficial, both to SMEs and to economic development. In India, such programs encouraged SMEs to become dependent on subsidies and inhibited their growth.

Policies that favor large firms. Many low-income countries continue to protect large public enterprise sectors despite the fact that these often crowd out private ventures and monopolize markets. Public policies can also protect large private enterprises by restricting competition and by imposing barriers to entry, subsidies and tax exemptions. In Senegal special exemptions restrict entry, while high effective rates of protection limit competition.

from contacts with suppliers and buyers that provide them with manufacturing know-how. In addition, these governments supported SMEs through innovative use of public investment programs, and through strengthening technology and training institutions, in active collaboration with small industry and farmers associations. This support supplemented but did not substitute for what the firms could provide either individually or collectively. It gave them the necessary infrastructure and easier access to credit and technological support from productivity centers. Governments also made a special effort to help exporting firms by facilitating access to inputs at world prices, access to export credit, export market development, and promotion of export-oriented ventures (box 2.13).

Government technological support came through institutions dealing with standards and quality control and from productivity centers and extension services that help firms adapt existing technologies and improve production and management routines, as in Hong Kong and Taiwan (China) (box 2.14). This is now being successfully tried in India under a technology development project, supported by the Bank Group, to redirect the activities of government research institutes from expensive basic or applied research development to activities of more direct operational relevance to businesses.

A similar approach is being adopted in the agricultural sector. Successful research and extension programs focus on services that the private sector is unable to supply, such as those relating to staple food crops and basic farming techniques, and on activities that encourage private input suppliers and agroprocessing companies, often the best source of specialized advice, particularly for cash crops.

Extension services have benefited from the involvement of producers cooperatives in service delivery. One model of public-private cooperation is the IDA-supported initiative by the National Federation of Central African Livestock Producers, a herders' association that was assisted in taking over the delivery of livestock services. The sale of veterinary drugs increased fivefold, reaching 80 percent of the target population. And the herders association has been transformed into a major service organization—a driving force for livestock development. Similar approaches in other agro-based industries could significantly improve the productivity and earnings capacity of most rural activities, while freeing government resources for use in other areas, such as strengthening the rural roads network.

The quality of the labor force also affects enterprise development. A well-trained labor force increases productivity, makes the shift into new areas of economic activity, and increases the pace of technology assimilation. In many countries, public training systems are overextended and divorced from the needs of the private sector. The most successful programs combine government resources and strengths in analyzing economywide information with better private capacity in managing specific programs to make training systems more responsive to the needs of the economy (box 2.15). Many countries could benefit from modernizing the technology curriculums in secondary schools and helping individuals and firms acquire specialized training abroad.

BOX 2.13 ENTERPRISE DEVELOPMENT THROUGH EXPORT PROMOTION

Access to inputs at world prices. Import restrictions, relatively high import tariffs, and taxes on domestic inputs often handicap exporters in low-income countries from competing with exporters from other economies who do not face similar restrictions and costs. These cost disadvantages are normally overcome through duty drawback, duty exemption, and tax rebate mechanisms. In China, a well-administered duty exemption system has assisted exporters in maintaining cost competitiveness by allowing easy access to imported inputs—exports under duty exemption arrangements accounted for 27 percent of total exports in 1991. In most African countries streamlining and adequately funding such programs to significantly reduce the costs incurred by exporters will increase export competitiveness.

Easy access to export credit. In most African countries, access to export finance would be facilitated if there were automatic access to export credit and rediscounting facilities for export orders backed by letters of credit; if export credit risk and commercial risk insurance were easily available; and if restrictions on issue and negotiability of trade financing instruments, such as bankers' and governments' trade acceptances, were eliminated to spur growth of market-based trade-financing mechanisms. By allowing exporters to retain all foreign exchange earnings and thus earn the full scarcity premium on foreign exchange, the cost of export finance can be reduced.

Market and product development. Most firms in low-income countries need but cannot fully afford specialized services relating to export market identification, product and process adaptation, and compliance with ISO 9000 standards. In India, IDA assisted firms in acquiring specialized services and in implementing export market development strategies. The assistance, on a cost-sharing basis, enabled beneficiary firms to register average export growth of more than 50 percent. A recent study by IDA—-Africa Can Compete—-has shown that poor product quality and production technologies are important constraints preventing African firms from exploiting U.S. demand for Afrocentric textiles and home products estimated at around $200 million annually. A product and technology development program of the type used in India could assist African firms.

Export-oriented joint ventures. Export trading companies in many East Asian countries have provided critical logistical, marketing, sales, technology, and financial services to producers selling to overseas buyers. Enabling the establishment and operation of joint-venture or wholly foreign-owned trading companies could help Africa's new entrepreneurs gain access to foreign markets being opened by reform. In addition, export-oriented joint ventures could be facilitated by eliminating investment restrictions and by offering special export incentives. In some instances, export-processing zones have proved effective as interim arrangements for providing exporters with reliable infrastructure and for establishing the credibility of government policies.

BOX 2.14 ENTERPRISE DEVELOPMENT THROUGH TECHNOLOGY SUPPORT

In the late 1960s the Taiwanese (China) bicycle industry was facing difficulties in competing in export markets. Indeed a number of companies went out of business. The Taiwanese government entrusted MIRL (Metallurgical and Industrial Research Laboratory), a non-profit, government-supported research institution, with developing and implementing a modernization program in collaboration with producers and the industry association. MIRL identified problems in materials, manufacturing, design, and standards. It then assisted the bicycle plants in three areas. Engineering modifications were made to improve product specifications, to standardize material utilization, and to raise quality control procedures. Production changes were introduced to increase the efficiency of manufacturing and assembly procedures and the interchangeability of components. And greater efforts were made to market the higher quality and safety standards of the bicycles in the United States.

The technology upgrading program, implemented in close collaboration with manufacturers, cut manufacturing time by as much as 40 percent, complied with safety regulations set by the U.S. Consumer Products Safety Commission, and shifted production to light-frame bikes. Bicycle exports grew from less than $3 million in 1970 to close to $200 million by the end of the decade.

Since then Taiwanese firms have maintained their export competitiveness and have moved up-market. At present, bicycle exports are more than $2 billion.

In contrast, Indian producers, who were bigger exporters than the Taiwanese in the 1960s, failed to upgrade their technologies. They continued to produce basic models, which were losing appeal in international markets. They lacked a technological support system. And they were unable to combine low labor costs with technology and product upgrading. As a result, India has lost market share. Bicycle exports languish at less than $100 million, even though India is one of the largest producers of bicycles in the world.

This example suggests that technology support can play a critical role in enhancing the competitiveness of firms. To be effective, however, it must be based on clearly identified and strong needs, quick government recognition of the need, a technologically competent and commercially oriented research and development institution, a well-integrated action plan that focuses on specific process and design problems of a large number of producers, and continuous interaction and feedback from producers, with industry associations playing an important coordinating role.

In general, government procurement policies can be designed to promote small and medium-size firms. Ten West African countries are using their public investment program to help their budding contracting industry—often the launching pad of large companies—by combining technical assistance and a prompt payment system with contracting out infrastructure maintenance and

BOX 2.15 TRAINING POLICY REFORMS IN TOGO

Until 1990, both public and private training programs in Togo were rigidly administered and inadequately financed. Both quality and efficiency were low. In 1990, the government reformed its policies on training and institutional development, aiming to build a flexible private-public training system that would be responsive to the country's economic demands, provide more practical training, and strengthen the theoretical content imparted during apprenticeship. By upgrading skills, the government hopes to attract foreign investment in labor-intensive light manufacturing and thereby reduce the economy's dependence on subsistence agriculture and on cocoa, cotton, and coffee. The reform includes:

■ Strengthening government's capacity to monitor and analyze labor markets in both the public and private sector, formal and informal, by analyzing existing data and conducting household surveys, periodic censuses in the urban and rural sectors, and profession-specific studies. The information generated would be analyzed and widely disseminated to schools, training centers, and employers.
■ "Twinning" managers and instructors with overseas training institutes.
■ Establishing a national training fund, administered by a private-public management committee, to allocate financial resources to public and private training projects that meet predetermined criteria.

investments that were previously carried out by the public sector. These efforts have also succeeded in providing, in a cost-effective way, infrastructure services to underserved small—rural and urban—localities. This program provides a model that many countries could replicate on a large scale (box 2.16).

The telecommunications sector has considerable potential potential for developing modern small and medium-size enterprises. New technologies allow telecommunication services to be unbundled. Such value-added services as paging, electronic mail, and database information services can be provided through franchising arrangements without substantial capital requirements. Even in basic telephone services, independent operators can compete with existing operators in such services as pay phones. In India, pay phones have been franchised to small private operators, who have substantially improved access to telephone services and boosted the collection rate for the utility.

Efficient infrastructure

The quality and adequacy of infrastructure services are important determinants of how successful firms are in delivering products and services of high quality, at low prices, and in the shortest possible time. Poor public infrastructure increases private costs and is a drag on market efficiency—by increasing

BOX 2.16 THE AGETIP MODEL, WORKING WELL

Under the Agences d'Exécution des Travaux d'Intérêt Public (AGETIP) model of contract management—first used in a Bank-sponsored project in Senegal—subprojects on large public works are carried out by small, dynamic firms in the private sector, rather than by (largely) inefficient public agencies. An added benefit is liberating project managers from much red tape.

AGETIP is a private, not-for-profit company that does general contracting for municipalities, ministries, and other public entities. It hires consultants to prepare designs and bidding documents and supervise works. It issues calls for bids, evaluates them, and signs the contracts. It also evaluates a project's progress, promptly pays contractors, and oversees the final reception of the works, adhering throughout to a set manual of procedures. In its first year of operation in Senegal, AGETIP executed $8 million of works through 119 subprojects, used 78 (mainly small or medium-size) contractors, and created almost 2,000 person-years of employment.

AGETIP owes its success first and foremost to its efficient private sector management team. This team takes pride in paying contractors in ten days rather than the 30 allowed or the months taken by public entities. AGETIP is also able to hold its overhead low by contracting for engineering consultants and others only as needed. Moreover, its legal status as a private company exempts it from the many and cumbersome bureaucratic procedures imposed on the public sector.

Because AGETIP hires local contractors, it has stimulated the development of local consulting industries. On its roster are 680 local contractors and 160 local consultants. Its success has spurred other agencies to improve their performance. In the public sector, the Senegalese minister of public works is considering setting up an AGETIP within his ministry, and the mayor of Dakar has contracted with AGETIP to execute projects financed from his own budget.

AGETIP's success in Senegal has led to the creation of similar agencies under World Bank projects in ten countries, including Benin, Burkina Faso, Mali, Niger, and Mauritania. The Mauritanian project proposes to disseminate information to local communities in order to increase their sense of responsibility toward project works and improve communication between the grassroots and local authorities. Before projects are presented for funding, affected communities will be consulted, particularly when projects concern such issues as garbage collection or sewer cleaning, where grassroots participation can make a large difference.

investment and transactions costs, increasing barriers to entry, reducing competitiveness, and restricting access to domestic and international markets. Small and informal enterprises, particularly in rural areas, are hurt most by the failure of public infrastructure. Unlike bigger firms, they cannot afford private investments needed to compensate for public failure.

As documented extensively in the World Bank's *World Development Report 1994,* low-income countries have improved the coverage of their infrastructure. But they are slipping behind middle-income countries and need to do much more—and quickly—if their firms are to compete in international markets (table 2.3). Unmet infrastructure needs are still considerable. Electric power has yet to reach most people. Demand for telecommunications to modernize production and integrate into global markets is far outstripping supply. And in rural areas, transport, water, sanitation, and education facilities are still poor—especially for women and children. Often past investments in infrastructure have not had the expected development impact because of inefficient and inappropriate investments by the public sector. Surveys of private firms consistently highlight infrastructure as a critical constraint to investment and profitability—and as an important variable in the investment decisions of foreign firms.

In Africa, the poor state of infrastructure continues to retard growth of the private sector and impose high transaction costs. Telecommunications coverage in Sub-Saharan Africa is among the lowest in the world—averaging 0.4 lines per 100 inhabitants, compared with 4 in Asia and 6 in Latin America. And government-owned telephone companies lack the resources to deliver the massive increases in telephone lines needed to accelerate growth and expand exports. Besides capacity constraints, poor service reliability imposes a burden on firms and results in lost opportunities. In Kenya, it has been estimated that unreliable telephone and telex services reduce foreign exchange earnings by 1–2 percent.

Performance in the power sector is also mixed. Some countries—such as Ghana, Malawi, and Togo—have managed to rapidly increase output. But others—such as Tanzania and Guinea—have had their power output stagnate.

TABLE 2.3 INFRASTRUCTURE COVERAGE IN LOW-
AND MIDDLE-INCOME COUNTRIES, 1975 AND 1990

	Low-income countries		Middle-income countries	
Sector	*1975*	*1990*	*1975*	*1990*
Power-generating capacity (thousand kilowatts per million persons)	41	53	175	373
Telecommunications (main lines per thousand persons)	3	6	33	81
Paved roads (kilometers per million persons)	308	396	1,150	1,335

Source: World Bank 1994e.

The share of households with electricity in Sub-Saharan Africa—only 5 percent of all households—remains among the lowest in the world.

Failures to achieve high generating efficiency and control system losses have combined with budget constraints to reduce access to electricity. It has been estimated that by spending $1 million to reduce line losses, many countries could save $12 million in generating capacity. For private firms, the cost of unreliable power and chronic shortages has been considerable. In Nigeria, because of poor reliability of publicly supplied power, most private firms have to invest in electricity generators—adding 10–25 percent to their machinery and equipment budgets.

National transportation systems also often fail to deliver the logistical support necessary for private firms to reach new markets. In Zambia, it has been estimated that poorly maintained roads add 17 percent to freight costs. As a result of poor operating efficiency of the rail system, freight rates in Africa are on average twice as high as those in Asia, and one and a half times those in Latin America. Despite high returns on road maintenance investments, neglect of maintenance in Sub-Saharan Africa has eroded almost $13 billion worth of roads—one-third of those built in the past 20 years. The high cost of sea and air freight services undermines the competitiveness of exports from Sub-Saharan Africa. For example, a container costs $200 to pass through Abidjan's port, compared with $120 in Antwerp, and much less in East Asia. The cost of air transportation in Africa is also much higher than in East Asia—often four times as much. The performance of national airlines has been dismal. With the exception of such carriers as Ethiopian Airlines and Air Zimbabwe, national carriers (Zambia Airways, Cameroon Air, Kenya Airways, and Nigeria Airways) continue to rack up large deficits.

In China and India, the demand for infrastructure services outstrips supply, constraining fresh domestic and foreign investments. Delays in the delivery of coal cost China an estimated $70 billion in 1992. To maintain its planned economic growth, China will need to spend more than $100 billion by 2000 to upgrade its overburdened transport system. In India, chronic power shortages often cripple industrial production and cause production costs to soar, while frequent voltage fluctuations or sudden disruptions in supply damage equipment. In 1992–93, power shortages, estimated at 18 percent of peak capacity requirements, resulted in low capacity utilization and substantial production losses. Equally disruptive is the inefficient management of transport services, which often raises operating and inventory carrying costs. Poor management of ports in India, for example, adds $80 to each container of Indian exports.

The problems of infrastructure detailed above stem from poorly specified goals, lack of managerial autonomy and accountability, chronic financial distress, price controls, insufficient competition, and wage and labor problems. As a result, governments in many low-income countries are increasingly taking a fresh, pragmatic look at expanding the menu of options for delivery of infra-structure services.

At the heart of these new approaches is greater involvement of the private sector, more decentralized and participatory approaches to public infrastructure investments and maintenance, and stronger capacity of the public sector to oversee and regulate private sector involvement. Governments recognize that technological, institutional, and regulatory innovations now allow competitive private delivery of many services. They are increasingly unbundling infrastructure services and applying a range of market options to increase efficiency, competition, and private investment.

The menu of options ranges from management contracts, leases, and concessions to outright sales of assets. These approaches are increasing competition from substitutes (for example, natural gas for coal). They are also increasing competition in and for the market. In many Sub-Saharan African countries, such port activities as stevedoring, tug-boat services, dredging,

---

Perhaps the greatest lasting benefit of private participation in infrastructure is that governments can increase the allocation of resources to areas crucial to the long-term growth of the private sector

---

and piloting are being handed over to the private sector. Viet Nam and Pakistan are considering leasing container terminals to private operators. In the water sector, concessions and leases to private operators are working well in Guinea and Côte d'Ivoire. In Sri Lanka and India, urban transportation has been deregulated to allow profitable operation of small vehicles by entrepreneurs. Private toll-road operations are planned in Ghana, India, and Pakistan. In countries as diverse as China, Ghana, Sri Lanka, and India, large parts of the telecommunications sector are being opened to private operators. In Sri Lanka, by 1993 four private cellular operators had been licensed—and competition between these operators has produced tariffs among the lowest in the world.

The power sector, particularly power generation, also has been opened to private participation in many countries. In Ghana and Guinea Bissau efforts are under way to bring in private firms under performance-based contracts, while in Tanzania and Côte d'Ivoire new projects will involve private investment. In Pakistan and India, private power generation in the form of independent power production is actively promoted and will contribute both to increasing efficiency and reducing the financial burden on governments. To stimulate this flow of private capital and management, many countries are revising their regulatory regimes and examining options for providing financial assurances to investors and lenders, often with help from IDA.

Besides new private investments, privatization of existing infrastructure utilities is an option available to low-income countries, particularly where the need to control persistent budget deficits leaves the public sector with limited resources for maintaining and expanding infrastructure capacity. In many middle-income countries, particularly in Latin America, privatization of infrastructure has been pursued to relieve overextended government budgets, improve operating efficiency, increase capacity, and reduce the cost of services to private firms. Infrastructure privatizations in developing countries mobilized about $25.4 billion between 1988 and 1993, of which $5.2 billion were raised through bond and equity sales in international markets (World Bank 1994e). The privatizations were mainly in the telecommunications and power sectors with Latin America, followed by East Asia, accounting for most of them (table 2.4).

Few low-income countries have yet pursued the privitization of infrastructure aggressively. In light of rapid changes in the infrastructure sectors in middle-income countries, low-income countries will have to step up their efforts to maintain the competitiveness of domestic firms and increase their access to international markets. True, the privatization of infrastructure in low-income countries poses special problems—embryonic domestic capital markets, limited domestic entrepreneurial capacity, weak regulatory mechanisms.

TABLE 2.4 INFRASTRUCTURE PRIVATIZATIONS IN DEVELOPING COUNTRIES, 1988–93

(percent)

	1988	1989	1990	1991	1992	1993
Region	100	100	100	100	100	100
Latin America	100	9	79	95	74	38
East Asia	0	91	20	4	25	25
Other	0	0	1	1	1	37
Sector	100	100	100	100	100	100
Telecommunications	75	9	94	90	35	35
Power	25	91	0	5	36	46
Gas	0	0	0	0	23	2
Other	0	0	6	5	6	17
Total (billions of dollars)	0.4	2.3	4.3	6.3	8.3	3.8

Note: Privatizations include sales in local markets and exclude airlines, shipping, and road transport.
Source: World Bank 1994d,e; Sader 1993.

But options to overcome these problems are being applied in some countries. These issues are discussed in detail in chapter 3.

Perhaps the greatest lasting benefit of private participation in infrastructure is that governments can increase the allocation of resources to areas crucial to the long-term growth of the private sector, but where private participation is often difficult. One is rural infrastructure, an area of considerable underinvestment in most low-income countries.

In Sub-Saharan Africa, the neglect of rural roads, education facilities, small-scale irrigation facilities, and telephone and power connections often cuts farmers and processors off from urban markets and from export markets. It also cuts them off from access to improved inputs, equipment, and technology. On average, road density is 34 miles per square kilometer in Africa, compared with more than 500 in India. In Cameroon, more than 80 percent of the unpaved road network—predominantly in rural areas—is in need of complete reconstruction and compaction. In India, it has been estimated that the decline in public investment in rural infrastructure during the 1980s led to a decline in the growth of private rural investment, from 2.8 percent a year in the 1970s to 1.9 percent in the 1980s.

Several low-income countries are attempting to redress the imbalance in infrastructure investment between rural and urban areas. In this effort, they are decentralizing implementation and relying more on community-based approaches to rural infrastructure development and maintenance—approaches that lead to better project effectiveness and resource mobilization. Ghana, for instance, has set aside 25 percent of its road funds for rural roads. In Ethiopia, a community organization, Gurage Road Construction, has mobilized resources for maintaining and improving more than 350 kilometers of roads. In Sierra Leone, Tanzania, and Zambia, district councils are taking on the responsibility for road maintenance.

These approaches, in tandem with greater private sector involvement, will permit increased spending on education at the primary and secondary levels and on primary health services—areas in which public investment in real terms has yet to climb back to levels of the 1970s. They will also permit governments in South Asia to tackle the massive problem of rural illiteracy.

The agenda for developing an attractive yet competitive business environment

In sum, the growth of a dynamic private sector requires a business environment that:

- Encourages and welcomes private entrepreneurship and reduces uncertainty and risks through continuity and consistency of policies.

■ Encourages market relationships through legal and judicial systems that protect property rights and provide a framework for their exchange.

■ Fosters competition through open, neutral, and nondiscriminatory policies for trade, regulatory, and investment.

■ Reduces transaction costs through simple regulations, well-managed institutions of public finance, and well-functioning infrastructure.

■ Commits governments to support enterprises through facilitation of trade and investment, innovative use of public investment programs, and investments in technology and skills development.

■ Forges lasting partnerships between governments and the private sector—with a view to overcoming private sector concerns about policy reversals and systematically eliminating impediments that the private sector views as most onerous.

Countries that have achieved this business-friendly competitive environment have done so through a determined effort by the government to develop competent and responsive institutions that work closely with private firms, labor organizations, and civic societies. The financial and technical assistance of the donor community can do much to support what must remain a local initiative and effort.

CHAPTER 3

Reforming public enterprise—farther and faster

POORLY performing public enterprises are a drain on the budget, a destroyer of banks, and an obstacle to private business. If low-income countries in Africa are to make a significant and rapid breakthrough into higher growth rates, if South Asian countries are to consolidate the gains they have made in liberalization, and if China is to maintain its rapid growth, they will all have to move farther and faster in solving the problem of public enterprises, especially the largest firms.

The choice is not a simple one between privatizing all public enterprises and reforming them without changing ownership. Simultaneous action is required on both fronts. But public enterprise reform is more effective—and more enduring—when the private sector is involved as manager, investor, financier, and increasingly as part owner. And liquidating industrial public enterprises that cannot be sold, but that persistently perform poorly, not only stops waste—but also gives the assets a chance for a second life. Admittedly, there are serious obstacles to privatization in low-income countries. But mechanisms to overcome them are being devised and deployed.

Even as the involvement of the private sector in public enterprises increases, the role of government remains crucial. Privatization, whether of management or ownership, yields substantial and enduring benefits—but only when it is done right. Doing it "right" means:

- Devising sector-by-sector policies.
- Introducing and maintaining competitive forces.

- Establishing and preserving a sound regulatory framework for the remaining monopolies, public and private.
- Maintaining transparency in transactions.
- Convincing investors that the probability of future expropriation is close to zero.
- Negotiating, monitoring, and enforcing contracts with private suppliers of management and financing.
- Devoting the resources from sales to productive uses.
- Managing the inevitable political and social tensions that arise as reforms in enterprises are implemented, especially the critical issues of foreign ownership and labor layoffs.

All these are largely a matter of government functioning in an effective and far-sighted manner. IDA has long provided member governments with assistance to improve policymaking and administrative functions. But these efforts will need to be redoubled as governments in low-income countries move from directly productive roles to those of conceiving, facilitating, and arbitrating.

Public enterprise reform is more effective—
and more enduring—when the private sector is involved
as manager, investor, financier, and increasingly as part owner

New in the equation is the realization that, even for donors, the task is not purely technical. The processes of adjustment and liberalization in general, and increased private participation in particular, have been poorly explained to the people whose lives are affected by these programs. Governments, with donor assistance, could do much more to make the public aware of the high cost people pay because of poor public enterprise performance. Governments should also calculate and make better known the price of inaction. And donors could spend more time describing the benefits of reform, not only to officials in ministries of finance, but also to legislators, academics, and opinion leaders. The process of privatization is inevitably intensely political. Where it has succeeded, it is because a consensus has been structured among enough interested parties to push it through (box 3.1).

The essential message of this chapter is that low-income countries cannot maintain "business as usual" for their public enterprises. Past reforms not involving private participation have produced only modest results. Privatization of a few small industrial firms—the standard approach in many low-income countries—has not had a major impact on the macroeconomic front. Nor has it served to signal government commitment to fundamental change and reform. Problems and losses in public enterprises continue to mount so rapidly that if they are not dealt with immediately, they will threaten or cancel most other reform efforts in many low-income countries. Nonetheless, there is reason for optimism. The perception of leaders and officials about the usefulness of public enterprises has changed greatly in the light of continuing poor performance.

BOX 3.1 PRIVATIZATION IN CAPE VERDE: A PARTICIPATIVE APPROACH

The government of Cape Verde has successfully mobilized public support for the need to reform its public enterprise sector and implement its divestiture program. This has been achieved by:

■ A well-conceived, aggressive, and sustained television and radio information campaign on the theme "Let's modernize Cape Verde," highlighting opportunities for higher growth led by the private sector.

■ The involvement of local consultants, alone or in joint venture with respected foreign firms, in designing the program and assisting in its implementation.

■ The sensitivity to local constraints and conditions and sense of ownership generated by the fact that the privatization agency is staffed entirely with Cape Verdean nationals, including one resident adviser of Cape Verdean origin.

Once the program got under way, public anxiety nonetheless built up regarding the impact of the program on an already difficult unemployment situation. In response, the government, with the support of IDA, organized a series of eye-opening visits to countries that had gone through a similar economic reform and opening-up process, such as Mauritius. Participation in these sensitization programs was targeted to such opinion leaders as journalists, union leaders, local elected officials, local business representatives, and key civil servants. During these trips, meetings and discussions were arranged with labor leaders, local entrepreneurs and foreign investors, managers of free-trade zones, and government officials in such ministries as justice, labor, industry, tourism, economy, and planning. The visits proved instrumental in convincing a large segment of the public of the potential of the reforms—and in rallying support for the necessary steps to complete them.

The privatization agency has tried at every step to ensure that the needed liquidations, restructuring, and privatizations are carried out with a minimum of labor unrest and social disruption. For instance:

■ Its approach to the whole process has been participatory, with constant efforts to involve the persons most affected (workers and managers) in the discussion of divestiture options.

■ Its creativity led to the design of socially acceptable solutions, mainly through the use of management-employee buyouts.

■ And its proactive provision of support to the newly privatized enterprises identified potential domestic and foreign sources of technical assistance and financing.

The way forward is:

- To sell what can be sold, particularly the large industrial firms formerly classified as strategic, the banks, and the functions of crop marketing boards and distribution companies.
- To involve the private sector as much as possible in enterprises in which outright sale is not (or not yet) feasible, particularly infrastructure firms and utilities.
- To redouble efforts to commercialize any remaining state-owned firms and strengthen government's essential supervisory and regulatory roles.
- To liquidate unsellable persistent loss-makers in the industrial sector.

None of this work will be easy. But, as will be shown, it is essential that steps be taken to stop the hemorrhaging of wasted resources.

Public enterprises are not performing well

Just about every developing country created public enterprises in the 1960s and 1970s. In low-income countries—where private sectors were smallest, weakest, and often least national in ownership—arguments for controlling the economy's "commanding heights" struck a particularly responsive chord.

The result: the number and economic importance of public enterprises became greater in low-income countries than in the rest of the developing world. In 40 developing countries, public enterprises account for 11 percent of GDP, 20 percent of total investment, and 5 percent of employment. But in the African countries in this group, they provide 14 percent of GDP, 27 percent of investment, and 18 percent of employment (World Bank 1995). What is alarming is that the share of public enterprises in economic activity correlates negatively with economic development.

Some public enterprises perform well, many more perform respectably, and many more could be made to perform acceptably. But it has long been apparent that their overall financial and economic performance has been inadequate. They make financial losses that deeply affect the state budget and in many cases contribute to the difficulties of the banking system. And they crowd out the private sector, in both product and financial markets, and generally increase the cost of doing business.

This situation, far from improving, is getting worse. To illustrate:

- In China, by government admission, up to 40 percent of the state-owned enterprises now make losses, with the total fiscal loss equivalent to some 3 to 5 percent of GDP, not counting losses in the banking system. The percentage of loss-making firms is mounting—despite a decade of reform efforts and high and sustained growth in the economy. Subsidies to the state enterprises topped an unsustainable 3.5 percent of GDP in 1993 (box 3.2).

- In Ghana, after a decade of effort on public enterprise reform, non-performing debts and unpaid corporate taxes of public enterprises come to about 3 percent of GDP. The minister of finance complained in November 1994 that "huge sums of taxpayers' money are placed at the disposal of the public sector annually without the money yielding any dividend."

- In Nigeria, nonperforming loans to public enterprises total more than $630 million. It has been estimated that the size, weight, and poor performance of the Nigerian public enterprise sector add 25 percent to the cost of doing private business in the country.

- In Burundi, over three years, total net flows from government to the public enterprise sector averaged 12.5 percent of government expenditure. Data from five other African economies show that total direct transfers from government to public enterprises accounted for 14–22 percent of expenditures. Indirect flows amounted to an additional 14 percent of expenditures (Sherif 1993).

If these outflows went to productive investments, they might be worthwhile. But this is seldom the case. The return on assets of public enterprise sectors in many low-income countries is negative and trending downward. And the losses on investment are large and growing.

These figures surpass cause for concern. They indicate that firms, sectors, and indeed some economies are in crisis. The problem is compounded by the generally low saving rates in most low-income countries: an average of about 12.5 percent in Sub-Saharan Africa and 23 percent in India, compared with 39 percent in China during 1987–93. In many cases in Africa, public enterprise losses just about cancel domestic savings, severely limiting government's capacity to provide social services. (Countries with a high saving rate retain some room to maneuver after covering public enterprise losses.)

Even where public enterprise losses are moderate and many public enterprises post profits, the return on capital invested in public enterprises is lower—often a third or less—than capital invested in similar operations run by the private sector. (For example, the rate of return on capital employed in Indian public enterprises has averaged about 2 percent.) And the average rate of return is almost always less than governments' cost of funds. The conclusion is inescapable: poor public enterprise performance is a major problem for most low-income countries—in Africa, South Asia, and the economies in transition alike.

Not enough commercialization

It is possible to make a public enterprise work well without changing its ownership. The likelihood is high that the profitability and efficiency of a public enterprise will increase:

- When it is assigned clear and unambiguous objectives in which commercial profitability features prominently.
- When competent management is given the full power to pursue these objectives—meaning that management is allowed to ignore noncommercial objectives that conflict with profitability, or that the firm is reimbursed transparently for the costs of fulfilling such objectives.
- When management is rewarded and sanctioned mainly on the basis of commercial performance.
- And especially when the enterprise is allowed to operate in a competitive market, without barriers to entry or exit.

BOX 3.2 CHINESE INDUSTRY MOVES TOWARD THE MARKET

China possesses more than 100,000 state-owned enterprises (SOEs). They account for 43 percent of production, employ more than 100 million people, yield in aggregate a positive return on capital—and are increasingly thought to be posing serious problems. Despite reform efforts, close to 40 percent—up from a third not long ago—make losses. They also burden the banking system: in mid-1993, SOEs commanded 70 percent of all loans from state banks, of which an estimated 15 percent (or some $40 billion) are nonperforming. China's State Economic and Trade Commission has concluded that as much as half the public industrial sector requires radical restructuring, and another third could be declared bankrupt. The causes of the problems are evident: SOEs are heavily burdened with social objectives, such as maintenance, housing, and clinics. Their managers lack autonomy. Reforms that might result in increased unemployment are resisted fiercely.

These enterprises co-exist with several types of collectively owned enterprises (COEs). Numbering more than 1.8 million and employing 112 million people (in 1993), they account for at least 40 percent of industrial production (while absorbing only 30 percent of domestic investment) and produce 25 percent of industrial exports. COEs are growing at an average rate of 30 percent a year and, along with other types of private firms and joint ventures, account for three-fourths of China's industrial growth. Owned by subnational governments or collectives, their focus is on profits, and they are much less burdened with social objectives. The local officials controlling them can appoint and dismiss managers, assume direct control, dispose of assets (sell or close the firm), and control residual income. Operating in competitive markets, they can and do go out of business.

COE managers are rewarded and penalized on the basis of performance. They have much greater freedom than SOE managers to hire

Adapting this package of commercialization reforms to local conditions and implementing them in a wide range of public enterprises formed the bulk of IDA's public enterprise reform efforts in the 1970s and early 1980s. And it continues as an important activity to this day in enterprises that, temporarily or indefinitely, will remain in the hands of the state (box 3.3). Commercialization is particularly applicable in low-income countries in transition, with their vast public enterprise sectors and difficulties in mounting rapid and mass privatization programs, and where the state typically remains as a major shareholder even after the first steps toward privatization. But experience clearly shows that successes in commercialization have been elusive—the record of reforming public enterprises without involving the private sector is largely unsatisfactory. Why is this so?

BOX 3.2 (continued)

and fire according to need and to make decisions on plant location, product lines, and prices. COEs rely heavily on retained earnings and private capital for their investment needs. They come closer to private firms than to public enterprises. But those who control them are not private owners in that they do not have title to the assets. Further, unlike private owners, there is a need to respond to community demands, such as a preference for employment maintenance over maximizing profits.

This midway position between public and private ownership would be difficult to replicate elsewhere. But evidence shows that COEs are performing much more productively than SOEs. A key reason is that the subnational governments and agencies that own the COEs rely crucially on the revenues they generate. Without COE profits, these governments would have no resources.

While many SOEs are creating less-constrained COEs and joint ventures, a massive amount of capital and labor (particularly in heavy industries) is still tied up and used inefficiently. The drag of the SOE sector could be tolerated during the recent period of high and stable growth, but the costs are greater and more evident in the current period of higher inflation—and threatening the health of the financial system. Recognizing these costs, the government is taking steps to:

■ Experiment with supervisory arrangements that give greater autonomy and more focused oversight to SOE managers.

■ Subject SOEs to market forces on both the debt and equity sides—by reducing guarantees, making SOEs compete for credit with nonstate firms, and floating minority shares of SOEs on stock exchanges inside and outside China.

■ Remove social obligations from the SOEs, and transfer them to subnational governments.

■ Impose a harder budget constraint on all SOEs.

■ Close or severely downsize the most hopeless performers.

Partial reform

The first problem lies in marshaling the will and resources to install the complex and often contentious commercialization reform package. Partial reform does not do the job. In Africa, in South Asia, and in many low-income countries in transition, the landscape is littered with inadequate, unsustained attempts of government owners to keep output prices at cost-covering levels, to lay off excess workers, to restructure the powers and composition of boards of directors, and to increase the autonomy of managers to hire, fire, locate plants, and choose suppliers.

Soft budgets

Attempts to impose a hard budget constraint on public enterprises have all too often proven ineffective. Early reforms often stopped unjustified direct transfers

---

BOX 3.3 BENIN'S BROADLY BASED PROGRAM OF PUBLIC ENTERPRISE REFORM

Benin's experience shows the benefits of using a wide range of reform measures to address the problems of a poorly performing public enterprise sector. In 1986 the country had about 60 parastatal entities, accounting for 75 percent of industrial production and monopolizing most productive subsectors, including manufacturing, agricultural processing, mining, and transportation. These entities employed 28,000 people and utilized 55 percent of all bank credit to productive firms in the country. Enterprise performance was poor, suffering from both overregulation and ineffective regulation, controlled prices, and lack of managerial autonomy.

But by the end of 1994, 32 enterprises remained in the government's portfolio, of which only 15 were commercial entities. Five more are scheduled to be divested in early 1995. In eight years, the number of firms has been cut by more than half. Employ-

ment in the sector has been reduced by about half. The percentage of total banking credit absorbed by public enterprises has declined to 18. The amount of enterprise debt guaranteed by government has fallen by 80 percent. And the turnover of privatized firms has more than doubled—from 9 billion CFAF in 1988 to 21 billion CFAF in 1993, indicating strong post-divestiture performance.

How did this come about? The government's reform program started in the mid-1980s when, alarmed by the increasing number of insolvent enterprises and the harm nonperforming debts posed to the banking system, IDA assistance was sought, and a program was adopted. Twenty-one loss-making operations were liquidated, including the airline, a textile corporation, and a freight firm. Six operations were sold (some with IFC involvement), including the brewery and a cement company. And ten operations to public enterprises from the budget. But they were quickly replaced by concessionary credits from the banking sector. When and where that flow has been turned off, public enterprises have still managed to receive credits from nonbank financial institutions—and went unpunished when they did not pay taxes, dividends, customs duties, suppliers, or each other. Enterprises usually register improved performance when forced to operate with retained earnings, with what they can borrow on strictly commercial terms without a government guarantee, and with what they can raise from the private sector in terms of joint ventures or equity.

The upshot: Implementing the entire reform package has proven just about as difficult, administratively and politically, as privatization itself. Governments tend to pick and choose from the package those elements they find tolerable. Reforms tend to be partial—and therefore inadequate. Research has shown that some of the public enterprise reform mechanisms used most heavily in the past are of dubious utility. A 1994 World Bank study, for exam-

---

BOX 3.3 (continued)

were subjected to restructuring measures, including management contracts for several hotels and increased rigor in the public investment review process. Although some of the liquidated firms were small, moribund units, the reform program as a whole has resulted in the withdrawal of the government from entire sectors of the economy, including imports, consumer goods distribution, transportation, brewing, and cement.

The removal of price controls, changes in the legal and regulatory frameworks, and major alterations to the banking sector, including the liquidation of the three former state banks and the introduction of private commercial banking, accompanied these divestiture measures. As downsizing produced layoffs, NGOs successfully launched a special program to generate jobs in small and medium-size private firms. These measures have set the conditions for the resumption

of private sector growth, as evidenced by the improved performance of the firms transferred to private owners.

Benin's program illustrates most of the reform principles and measures espoused in this chapter. It attacked simultaneously enterprise reform and privatization. It took extensive and bold steps to liquidate persistent losers. It sold or closed firms that couldn't be sold immediately. It combined enterprise reforms with far-reaching financial sector reforms (including liquidation and reliance on new private entrants). And it made a concerted effort to make the transition palatable to those most directly affected. The next step in the process should be to expand privatization into the infrastructure fields—areas that still remain under state control (for an example of how this is being done elsewhere in Africa, see box 3.7 on the electricity sector in neighboring Côte d'Ivoire).

ple, reviewed 12 agreements laying out the mutual obligations and responsibilities of the owner (the state) and public enterprise managers. It concluded that they did little to improve performance and in some cases may have contributed to performance declines (World Bank 1995).

Backsliding

Even in the few cases where the whole package of reforms is put in place, it tends not to stay in place—for backsliding is frequent. The common story is that bad times make for good policy. In crises, especially financial crises, governments muster the will to install tough reform packages that establish the precedence of commercial objectives, impose a hard budget constraint, reduce excess work forces, give managers the autonomy to achieve commercial aims, and pay them according to their performance.

But once the crisis fades, commitment fades with it, and the reforms are diluted or shelved—meaning that cost-cutting measures are stopped or reversed. For instance, Pakistan pioneered a system in the 1980s to measure industrial public enterprise performance each year and reward management for goal achievement—and for a time it produced positive results. But in 1993, supervisory officials indicated that the system was no longer being energetically applied. The conclusion: Even when not partial, reforms tend not to endure. While retreat from reform has also occurred in richer countries, backsliding has been both more common and more devastating in low-income countries, with their larger public enterprise sectors.

Turning to the private sector—slowly

Industrial and middle-income countries have had considerable success changing the ownership structure of public enterprises and involving the private sector directly in the construction, management, financing, and increasingly the partial or complete ownership of public enterprises. Low-income countries, too, have planned and embarked on a range of similar activities—but so far in a more restrained and limited manner and with far more limited results. In Kenya, only 5 of 200 public enterprises designated for privatization in 1991 had been sold by the end of 1993. In Bangladesh, of 40 firms slated for sale in 1991, only 9 had been privatized as of March 1994. And while 29 reforming African countries have privatized a fifth of their nearly 3,000 public enterprises, the economic weight of those sold—measured by turnover, investment, or employment—was far lower. Privatizations almost everywhere take longer than planned. And many countries have scaled back optimistic ambitions in light of experience. But the process has been even slower and more problem-filled in low-income countries, where caution, slippage, and delays in both enterprise reform and private sector development programs are common.

The reasons lie in a series of vicious circles common and powerful in low-income countries. Because private sectors were weak, governments pinned their hopes on public firms. But as the shortcomings of public enterprises have become more evident, there still is no private sector of sufficient size, experience, and wealth to turn to—in large part because of the emphasis placed on public enterprises. Because the bulk of credit has been directed from state-owned banks to state-owned firms, capital markets suffered relative neglect. Now that divestiture is on the agenda, few low-income countries have more than embryonic equity markets (though, encouragingly, these are on the rise in a range of low-income countries: for example, China, India, Kenya, Pakistan, Sri Lanka, and Zimbabwe).

Public enterprises have provided bureaucrats, politicians, and regime loyalists with income supplements, power, and myriad opportunities for illegal gain

---

Policymakers in some low-income countries are reluctant to privatize or increase the role of the private sector because they mistrust the managerial capacity of the public sector. They resist private involvement and divestiture because they have little faith in the capacity of the public administrative system to conduct transparent transactions, to regulate private monopolies, to collect corporate taxes on privatized firms, and to adjudicate disputes and enforce contracts. Thus, the managerial weakness of the state is cited, paradoxically, to justify the state's continued direct involvement in managing productive entities.

The dominance of the state in the economy means that few good employment opportunities exist outside the state structure. And people within the state apparatus often lack the experience and skills that open doors in the private sector. Moreover, public enterprises have provided bureaucrats, politicians, and regime loyalists with income supplements (sitting fees for board membership, for example), power (to obtain and hand out jobs), and myriad opportunities for illegal gain. Those being asked to diminish state dominance are precisely those who will pay a high and direct material price if the policies are applied. Even when bold leaders overcome all these problems and put forward a comprehensive reform package, they frequently find they are not supported—administrative institutions are weak and understaffed, and implementation capacity is lacking. So, the reform founders.

It is hard in low-income countries to find a catalytic core of people not dependent economically on the state. In middle-income and industrial countries, state-diminishing reforms have been led by political figures relying on stakeholders whose economic base lay outside the state structure—on economic actors who saw the advantages of less-fettered private initiative. And in transition economies, radical reformers were able (at first) to tap a large vein of antistate sentiment because the previous regimes were seen as foreign, repressive, or both.

Given the lack of a popular base with the power, the will, and the means to support reforms, liberalizing reformers in low-income countries have been fewer, their task more difficult, and their voices more muted. Workers and farmers, who will eventually reap the benefits of liberalization, are dispersed and unorganized. And their enthusiasm for the reforms is usually minimal—often because the benefits of reform are not fully passed on to them but siphoned off along the way. For the average citizen, the costs of reform are apparent and immediate, the benefits uncertain and future. All this means that reform and privatization are hard to sell (but see box 3.1).

The upshot of all this is a major development dilemma. Low-income countries have the greatest need for increased private sector involvement in their enterprises. But the factors that produce that need are those that make it difficult to launch, hard to implement, and hard to bring to fruition.

The picture is not uniformly bleak. Some governments—often with the assistance of IDA operations—have applied the commercialization package of public enterprise reforms more rigorously than in the past (see box 3.3). And while efforts to involve the private sector in public enterprises have been difficult to launch in low-income countries, they have by no means been entirely absent. Many public enterprise sales have been completed in Benin, Mozambique, Nicaragua, Nigeria, Senegal, Sri Lanka, Togo, and other low-income countries. Low-income countries actually pioneered some of the cutting-edge developments in infrastructure privatization outside Europe. For 30 years, the water supply of Abidjan in Côte d'Ivoire has been successfully managed by a private firm. Concession operations of this nature—now once again very much in favor worldwide—are in existence or in the advanced planning stage in several other low-income countries, including Cape Verde and Guinea.

What this shows is that the question for low-income countries is not what should be done—the "what" is fairly well known. The key question for low-income countries is "how":

- How to apply more widely the methods and techniques working well elsewhere and already showing promise in low-income settings.
- How to protect the private investor against government's changing the rules halfway through the game.
- How to build up the regulatory and guardian institutions to protect the public against the abuse of private economic power.

■ How to garner broadly based support, or at least build a powerful coalition of reformers, to initiate and push through reforms long enough to show positive results.

The way forward—farther and faster

A striking fact emerging from reform experience in the past few years is that public enterprise reform and divestiture should not be "either-or" pursuits. Countries undertaking serious commercialization efforts also tend to have serious privatization programs. This is as true outside low-income countries (Chile, Mexico, and New Zealand) as in them (Benin and Mauritania). The distinction is not between privatizers and nonprivatizers—it is between reformers and nonreformers.

Combining this insight with the pressing financial weight of so many public enterprises yields the idea that past public enterprise reform strategies and tactics in low-income countries have been too timid. What is needed now is to go forward much farther and much faster on five related fronts:

*Public enterprise reform and divestiture
should not be "either-or" pursuits*

■ Sell the public enterprises producing tradables or operating in competitive and potentially competitive markets—particularly banks and the large commercial firms previously classed as strategic.
■ Liquidate (but only after attempts to sell have failed) persistent loss-makers in industry and commerce.
■ Involve the private sector in the management, the financing, and as much as possible the ownership of infrastructure firms, especially the largest ones with the greatest economic weight.
■ Commercialize the remaining public infrastructure enterprises.
■ Strengthen legal systems and regulatory policies and institutions to set good policy, enhance competition, maintain transparency, provide investors with a stable and predictable environment, and protect the public interest.

The essential point is that only by going beyond the divestiture of small and medium-size public enterprises in manufacturing and services—and by privatizing large commercial firms and changing fundamentally the performance of public infrastructure enterprises—will low-income countries generate the savings and resources, and open the space for private economic activity, needed to break out of the economic stagnation afflicting so many of them.

That the heart of the financial problem lies in the largest firms is exemplified by Bangladesh, where just five public firms—the power corporation, the railways, the steel corporation, the Jute Corporation, and the Jute Mills Corporation—accounted in 1993 for more than 80 percent of the public sector's gross losses. In Nigeria the ten largest public enterprises account for more than 70 percent of the stock of outstanding government loans to the sector, and in Tanzania, for about 55 percent of total public enterprise debt. In Kenya between 1990 and 1992, direct and indirect subsidies to five large public enterprises averaged 2.7 percent of GDP each year. In short, in too many low-income countries the losses of a few large public enterprises impede if not paralyze most other government action. By addressing the problems of the largest firms low-income countries will free the space needed for private entry—and generate the resources required for avoiding reversal on the macroeconomic policy front and for creating and expanding social services.

Low-income countries are not middle-income countries and the policies and programs that worked well in a middle-income setting do not necessarily produce the same results at the same speed

---

The objective for low-income countries is to emulate the successes of such Latin American reformers as Argentina. Large-scale and rapid privatization of both management and assets generated revenues for the state. It reduced the government's foreign and domestic debt. It contributed to the decline of interest rates. It helped attract new private investment. And it led directly to increased government spending on health and education. Moreover, privatized infrastructure firms in Latin America have generally provided more and better services contributing to people's well-being and enticing more investors.

The problem is that Angola is not Argentina, Chad is not Chile, Malawi is not Mexico—low-income countries are not middle-income countries, and the policies and programs that worked well in a middle-income setting do not necessarily produce the same results at the same speed. The special problems of low-income countries mean that governments, donors, and private investors have to be more careful and more innovative than elsewhere. This point is legitimate. But recent experience demonstrates that even governments and economies in great difficulty can be turned around quickly. Less than a decade ago, the chances for fundamental reform in Argentina, Mauritius, and Mexico were regarded as slight, but their improvements of fortune were both large and swift. It is also clear that the privatization of medium-size, and even larger, enterprises producing tradables could be speeded up appreciably in many low-income countries—with four "ifs":

- If barriers to purchase by noncitizens or by citizens of a supposedly "wrong" ethnic group were reduced or eliminated.
- If governments set more reasonable floor prices for the firms being divested and accepted that some past investments in public enterprises are now worthless and should be liquidated.
- If there were heavier reliance on the private sector in the privatization process (to handle preparation and implementation) to minimize bureaucratic reluctance or outright resistance to privatization.
- If the concept of strategic enterprises were redefined or discarded.

But many low-income governments have been reluctant to open their privatization markets to foreign investors or to citizens of immigrant stock (for example, Asians in East and Central Africa)—and sometimes to citizens of a particular region or of a supposedly "advanced" or "favored" ethnic group.

In many low-income countries, governments set floor prices for their public enterprises based on accounting values that bear little relation to the market value of the business. And they resist or delay the termination of persistent loss-makers. Nigeria, for instance, withdrew 26 industrial enterprises from its 1989 privatization program because "they were in such poor shape that no one would invest in them except perhaps to strip them of their assets." Certainly, the liquidation of 26 firms would have been painful for Nigeria, as it is the world over. To be taken into account, however, are not only the political costs of a liquidation, or the acceptance of a low price, but the financial and opportunity costs of continuing inaction. What has it cost Nigeria to keep open, for five more years, 26 enterprises in evidently deplorable condition? To what better uses could those resources have been applied?

Liquidation—unsavory but essential

The economics of bankruptcy are impeccable. But the prevailing attitude toward the liquidation of persistently loss-making companies is nearly always and everywhere purely negative, to the point where closures and liquidation are generally regarded as more difficult and time consuming and less palatable than privatization. In Guinea, 28 industrial public enterprises were privatized as part of an IDA program in the mid-1980s. Most of them promptly failed, and in a few years only five of the divested 28 were still in operation.

Many interpreted this heavy failure rate as a disastrous outcome. But was it? The firms had been loss-makers for some time, and they had survived only because of protection, tax exemptions, and other subsidies. The government had not been able to muster the will to restructure successfully or to close these uneconomic ventures. But once they were in private hands, and it was clear that a change of ownership was not sufficient to let them survive in the marketplace, the firms were allowed to go under—to "exit." If the firms had not been sold, they would—as public enterprises—probably still be alive today, racking up losses, receiving subsidies, and draining the Guinean economy. So, privatization allowed the government to step away from persistent losers. While it would have been politically preferable for the privatized firms to have survived and flourished, at least the drain of public resources was stopped.

Liquidation of chronic loss-makers has to be seen not as the death but as the rebirth of previously nonperforming assets

The survival of only 5 of 28 divested firms raises the fear that privatization might lead to deindustrialization in low-income countries. But no country, and surely no low-income country, can afford to subsidize losers perpetually. Liquidation of chronic loss-makers has to be seen not as the death but as the potential rebirth of previously nonperforming assets—since those still of value are auctioned off and put to alternative and, it is hoped, better use. The reduced drain on government could lead to better policies, to improved social services, to a better climate for investment and business, and eventually to better growth.

Moreover, the technological and organizational revolution now under way is based not on large, capital-intensive industrial firms (of the type so often in difficulty in public sectors in low-income countries) but on small and medium-size firms—labor intensive in nature, with quick start-up times and agile responses to rapidly shifting markets and technologies. In a number of sectors in low-income countries private firms have led the way—in Bangladesh (garments), India (software), Kenya (cut flowers), and Mauritius (garments and electronics). The widespread application of this approach can produce more plants, jobs, and exports than the overcapitalized, protected, and inefficient large public enterprises that will inevitably leave the ranks of the public sector.

Privatizing privatization

Many low-income countries have problems in organizing and administering the privatization process. A prime source of delays has been institutional deficiencies, as inexperienced and unmotivated civil servants either have difficulty or take a great deal of time to carry out preparatory measures. A good way to overcome this problem is by using the private sector to handle most of the implementation (but not the policy) steps. This has been done with great success in settings as varied as Mexico, Morocco, and Russia—and is now being applied in Ghana. This approach has the additional payoff of promoting local consulting and analytical capacity, as foreign consultants and investment banks normally rely heavily on local counterparts. Again, the need to move to the divestiture of the largest firms is highlighted, because while it might be difficult to attract large foreign services for the privatization of very small companies, the sale or leasing of large manufacturing or infrastructure enterprises will definitely attract the larger, more experienced foreign firms.

New methods of sale

What is very important for low-income countries is that privatization mechanisms now exist that simultaneously address two critical problems. The first is putting the assets in the hands of more competent, properly motivated managers. The second is giving an ownership stake to the local population to show them that privatization is not just for the benefit of the foreign investor or the local elite. These mechanisms combine the sale of a controlling stake to an experienced, core investor—who brings in capital, managerial talent, access to markets, and new technology—with devices that spread shares widely among the local population.

The mechanisms work in low-income countries. In Sri Lanka, more than 30 industrial and manufacturing public enterprises, some of significant size, have been sold by the negotiated sale of a majority stake to a core, qualified investor, foreign or domestic—and the donation of 10 percent of shares to the workers—followed by sequenced sales of remaining shares on the local stock exchange, with incentives for small and first-time purchasers.

Where local stock exchanges are nonexistent or weaker than in Sri Lanka, interim institutions—such as the Zambian Privatization Trust Fund (box 3.4)—can speed the transfer of a majority stake, remove the remaining shares from direct government control, and start developing the equity market. And one low-income country in transition, Mongolia, pioneered the use of vouchers, which gave citizens purchasing power and allowed them to participate in the mass privatization of the public enterprise sector.

Despite consideration in a few preliminary studies (in Ghana and Tanzania), a voucher scheme has yet to be applied in other low-income countries. A primary impediment is the lack of a complete registry of the citizenry. Bolivia, with the help of IDA, is launching an ambitious capitalization program that will put half the equity of its six largest public enterprises into private hands, with the remaining half going to a group of private pension funds owned by the citizens of the country (box 3.5). Bolivian authorities are finding registration to be a problem, but efforts are under way to overcome it. More devices of this nature will spring up soon in other low-income countries, with IDA support.

BOX 3.4 THE ZAMBIAN PRIVATIZATION TRUST FUND

Created as part of an IDA-supported reform program, the Zambian Privatization Trust Fund holds for future sale to small Zambian investors blocks of shares in companies in which 51 percent or more of the equity has been sold to core investors. If fund managers consider the minority shares offered to them by the government an unsound investment, they are free to reject them. Once the shares have been transferred to the fund, the government is no longer allowed to vote them but still collects dividends and proceeds from share sales.

The fund's main purpose is to develop the equity market and stimulate share purchase by local investors. It issues shares through public offerings and financial intermediaries, offering deep discounts and establishing ownership limits to avoid large concentrations. Small investors receive encouragement to retain their shares.

The members of the fund's board of trustees are drawn from the banking sector, the Zambia Chamber of Commerce, the Law Association of Zambia, and private persons and entities. The fund will be managed by the private professional management company that wins a competition for the contract. The selection process will be supervised by the board of trustees. The contract is structured so that fund management has an incentive to dispose of—not hold or manage—the portfolio. If all shares have not been sold at the end of five years the fund will be converted into a unit trust and offered to Zambian investors. If there are few takers, remaining shares could be distributed free to Zambian citizens.

Larger industrial public enterprises

Using such methods can speed the sale of small and medium-size industrial firms, but what about the larger industrial public enterprise firms, many formerly classed as strategic—steel mills, fertilizer companies, cement plants? As the limits on the managerial and financial capacity of the state have become more evident, the concept of strategic enterprise has narrowed and in many instances vanished. Many of these large firms can also be moved and should be moved to the sales block—if there is reasonable assurance that competitive forces can be brought to bear on them.

But governments in low-income countries have resisted the sale of such firms. They argue that their operation in monopolistic markets means that privatization would merely transform a publicly owned, constrained monopoly into a privately owned, unconstrained monopoly. Efficiency might rise, but people's well-being would decline. Moreover, even when the principle of divestiture of large firms is accepted, it is often accompanied by plans to restructure the entity before sale, ostensibly to increase the purchase price.

BOX 3.5 BOLIVIAN INFRASTRUCTURE GOES PRIVATE—PART WAY

With IDA assistance, Bolivia is transferring into private hands half the ownership and all the management of the six largest public enterprises in the country—the railway, the airline, electricity generation and distribution, telecommunications, the hydrocarbons company, and the mining smelters. New international partners will invest in the companies rather than buy assets and in this way can acquire up to half the equity in each firm. While this will generate capital for investment-starved firms, the government will receive no revenues from the transactions and could incur substantial short-term costs. Core investors will sign management contracts containing an option to purchase additional shares when the contract expires. The other half of the equity will be held by five to ten newly created private pension funds serving all 3.2 million adult Bolivians. Proceeds from these managed funds will pay shareholders retirement and disability benefits.

IDA is supporting this program through adjustment and technical assistance operations designed to strengthen the Ministry of Capitalization, establish a regulatory framework for the privatized utilities, and begin capitalizing the Bolivian national telecommunications and airline companies.

The power of the first argument is declining. Adjustment programs in low-income countries over the past decade have set macroeconomic frameworks in order and liberalized the trade and fiscal regimes. These reforms increase the competitiveness and contestability of markets, making it more likely that privatized firms will face competition.

Many low-income countries, especially those in transition, are deeply attracted to the idea that industrial public enterprises, particularly the largest, could and should be restructured before sale. Restructuring is a broad term. When it consists of defensive or passive measures, such as labor-shedding before privatization (box 3.6), or changes in management and organization, or even settling some of an enterprise's debt, it is acceptable—even though some governments have left all these tasks to the new private owners. What is unacceptable is making new physical investments to boost value before the change of ownership.

New physical investments seldom add enough value to recover their cost. Most often, governments would have been financially better off selling at a lower price. Moreover, physical restructuring in a large firm is inevitably a long process. A growing body of evidence indicates that delaying privatization leads to further deterioration of the assets, decreased revenue for the state, and probably decreased welfare and efficiency for the economy.

The financial and economic costs of not privatizing can thus be very high. So even the large-scale public enterprises producing tradables should be sold—

BOX 3.6 LABOR RETRENCHMENT: A SLOW AND DIFFICULT JOB

India. Because a fear of labor retrenchment was holding back reform of India's huge public enterprise sector, IDA introduced a Social Safety Net Sector Adjustment Program in 1992. The National Renewal Fund, established to help workers affected by adjustment, includes an Employment Generation Fund (EGF) and a National Renewal Grant Fund (NRGF). The EGF finances the delivery of labor counseling, retraining, and redeployment services and area regeneration schemes that create jobs and use newly acquired skills.

Five agencies (including two private entities) are now in charge of EGF programs. Located in cities where major industrial restructuring is taking place, these agencies have conducted surveys of retrenched workers, regional labor markets, and training institutes—information that helped India devise detailed actions now being implemented.

The NRGF finances severance payments to retrenched workers. By March 1994, it had compensated roughly 66,000 retrenched workers from 67 public enterprises—less than the 80,000 targeted in NRGF's Business Plan for fiscal 1992 because industrial restructuring has been slow. These achievements are commendable, however, given that labor retrenchment in India was, until recently, entirely taboo.

Bangladesh. In Bangladesh, labor retrenchment has also been a contentious issue. New owners of privatized enterprises had been required to retain workers for at least one year after privatization. With these restrictions now removed, efforts are being made to retrench as much surplus labor as possible before privatization—usually through voluntary departure schemes based on generous severance benefits.

Severance benefits for all public sector employees were substantially

---

once it is clear that competition is present or imminent—and there should be no physical restructuring or new investments before sale.

Divestiture of utilities

What about utilities, the natural monopoly infrastructure service providers? Until recently, these have not been on the divestiture agenda in most low-income countries. But that is now changing. In telecommunications and electricity generation, technology has changed and introduced competition into areas and markets formerly closed. Organizational changes to enhance competition—such as vertical or horizontal unbundling of formerly integrated networks—open the door to increased private participation in many infrastructure firms.

In low-income countries, the privatization of a few utilities, or the heavy involvement of the private sector, would have a large impact on the budget. If experience elsewhere is a guide, it would increase the quantity and quality of

BOX 3.6 (continued)

increased in July 1989. A public enterprise employee with 30 years of service, for example, could be entitled to five years' pay. Training and job-search services also are being provided. The response has been encouraging. In public jute mills, about 18,000 workers applied for voluntary separation during fiscal 1991–93.

The recently approved, IDA-supported Jute Sector Adjustment Project will develop training and self-employment schemes to be administered by nongovernmental organizations (NGOs) and existing government training mechanisms. A reputable NGO will be contracted to act as principal coordinator for delivering training services and to establish a Jute Training Resource Center, with training facilities to be located in areas with a concentration of jute mills. Employees will have the choice of participating in several months of skills training or taking a self-employment course and receiving guaranteed loans to partially finance the set-up of businesses.

Cape Verde. An IDA project sponsoring technical assistance for privatization in Cape Verde helps match retrenched labor with demand in the private sector. The project helps former employees set up their own businesses, subsidizes the costs of retraining retrenched public employees incurred by their new employers (up to 40 percent of the employee's salary for six months), and financially supports the organization of private training workshops and evening courses. So far, the project has financed the retraining costs of 150 retrenched employees, who were subsequently hired by private companies. Progress has therefore been slow, but the program works. Once it is properly advertised, it should expand its operations.

service. It would stimulate local shareholding and capital markets—and signal the domestic and foreign private sector about the seriousness of government's intent. And it could slow or stop the hemorrhaging of resources and increase domestic savings. Even in the least developed settings where the asset value of major utilities is sometimes low, the franchise value remains substantial.

Telecommunications is a likely priority candidate—for several reasons. In a large number of low-income countries the demand for phone services is unfilled. Governments can no longer meet investment needs. Overstaffing is less of a problem in this sector than in others, and the likelihood is good that expansion, and perhaps even increased employment, will follow sale. Considerable know-how on telecommunications divestiture has been built up in the past five years in the business community and in the governments of low-income countries. Above all, international investors continue to be interested in acquiring stakes in telecommunications firms in emerging markets. Sales of such firms in Argentina, Chile, Mexico, and Venezuela have produced a stream of positive benefits and account for about half the capitalization of the stock exchanges in those countries. Low-income countries are starting to follow this trend, with partial sales of telecommunications already completed in Pakistan and under way in Bolivia, Burundi, Sri Lanka, and Tanzania.

There are two issues for increasing private participation in utilities in low-income countries. First, how will countries regulate portions of privatized (or partly privatized) infrastructure that cannot be subjected to competitive forces in the marketplace? Institutional and legal deficiencies make regulation onerous. Second, how can private investors be assured that government will maintain policy and pricing frameworks for them to earn a reasonable return on their investment? Investors want stable and predictable business environments, something in short supply in many low-income countries.

The two questions are related, and so are the answers. First, with changing technology the experience from privatization efforts around the world is that many fields of infrastructure can be subjected to some form of competition. So, the scope and need for direct government regulation have been reduced. Second, in recent years there have been promising experiments with tailoring market structure and regulatory choices to institutional capabilities. But there still is much to learn. One option, as yet untested, may be to contract out some regulatory functions. Building credibility in pricing and policy frameworks is likely to take time. Various approaches may be possible in the transition to enhance credibility of the government's commitment. An innovative approach may be recourse to foreign arbitration for dispute settlement. For example, the private operator of the Jamaica telecommunications company can appeal contract disputes to a U.K. court—but this approach may not be easily replicated. Multilateral institutions like the World Bank Group can also provide guarantees against the failure of governments to live up to their policy frameworks.

Privatizing management—and beyond

The economic and business uncertainty in many countries means that buyers will be hesitant and governments will be judged incapable of creating and maintaining a proper regulatory framework. And some governments will remain adamant that outright sale would pose intolerable political problems. In these cases, consideration can go to privatizing management without fully or immediately privatizing ownership. This solution is most appropriate for infrastructure firms operating in monopolistic markets. Methods to privatize management include management contracts, leases, concessions, and franchises.

A recent Bank study shows that in two-thirds of 20 cases reviewed, management contracts improved performance (World Bank 1995). But their use has been concentrated in a few sectors (hotels, agroindustries), and they place great demands on governments in devising, implementing, and monitoring the contracts—and leases and concessions, even more so. Nonetheless, the privatization of management retains its attraction in low-income settings—particularly in infrastructure enterprises, where the need for improved performance is overwhelming—since both government sensitivities and investor wariness are especially high. Between 1988 and 1994, IDA supported 23 operations to privatize management, most of them in the past few years. Sectors and countries included airlines (Cameroon and Chad), telecommunications (Guinea), power (Côte d'Ivoire, Guinea, Mali, Rwanda, and Sierra Leone), railways (Burkina Faso, Cameroon, India, and Tanzania), and solid waste management (Benin, Burkina Faso, Ghana, and Tanzania). For an example from the power sector, see box 3.7. The mechanism is not limited to infrastructure firms. In Guyana, a management contract dramatically improved the performance of a major bauxite mining operation.

The beneficial impact of privatizing management is greatly enhanced when the management provider takes an equity stake—or at least takes direct collection risk

---

The beneficial impact of privatizing management is greatly enhanced when the management provider takes an equity stake—or at least takes direct collection risk. A variation on this theme is the lease with an option to buy an ownership stake—partial or majority. In several World Bank infrastructure projects under preparation (telecommunications in Jordan, water in Trinidad and Tobago), private providers assume responsibility not simply for management but also for a percentage of needed investments during the period of the contract. The contractors have the option of becoming owners of the entity at the expiration of the contract. If they choose to exercise the option, the price of the investments is converted to equity, and World Bank guarantees provide assurance that the government will maintain its commitments. The familiarization period allows the government to examine the benefits of improved performance—and the investor to test government policies and price schedules. This approach can also be used for large-scale industry and for banks, both in great need of reform in almost all low-income countries.

These management and ownership approaches could and should be applied much more widely in low-income countries (for an example from a low-income country in transition, see box 3.8). In these operations, as in Côte d'Ivoire, IDA can provide more than finance for the rehabilitation of infrastructure. It also can provide technical assistance to improve government operations. Comfort levels of private managers and investors can be raised by the

---

BOX 3.7 PRIVATE PARTICIPATION IN CÔTE D'IVOIRE'S POWER SECTOR

Before private participation. In the 1970s and 1980s, Energie Electrique de Côte d'Ivoire (EECI) built the most extensive power grid in West Africa. Total capacity reached 850 megawatts. But its hydropower plants were poorly designed, its thermal units were not well maintained, and the power system never performed close to full capacity. Moreover, as economic decline set in in the mid-1980s, EECI was hit by budget cuts, bringing weaknesses in financial management to the fore. By 1990, the company was carrying large arrears on accounts receivable and debt in excess of one year's revenue. Losses were more than one-third of revenues.

The lease. In 1990 the government decided to lease the sector's assets to a private firm, Compagnie Ivoirienne d'Electricité (CIE), with 51 percent of the equity (CFAF 10 billion) held by a joint venture of the French utility companies, SAUR and EdF International. The rest of the equity was held by the government until it could be sold to local investors and company employees. At the outset, average power prices were reduced by 10 percent to CFAF 44 per kWh ($0.16)—still high by international standards and a major contributing factor to the country's high factor costs. Following the 50 percent devaluation of the CFA franc in January 1994, prices were adjusted to CFAF 53 per kWh ($0.09)—close to the average price in OECD countries and the long-run marginal cost of power in Côte d'Ivoire.

Efficiency gains. Observers calculate that while the cost of the concession was high, it was more than offset by efficiency gains. Since the introduction of the lease, system power losses have fallen from more than 20 percent to about 17 percent, and average outage time from 50 to 18 hours per system failure. And collections have risen to 98 percent of billings. In addition, the number of employees has dropped from 9.5 per 1,000 customers to 6.9, and revenues have

---

traditional mechanism of lending to the government, increasingly in support of or in conjunction with private investors.

The path for donors

Donors have to tread a narrow path between helping a government undertake painful reform and providing a government with the means to avoid or delay reform. A 1994 study of privatization in Sub-Saharan Africa argued that aid flows often "delayed rather than promoted" public enterprise reform and privatization (Berg 1994). The report was particularly critical of recapitalizations of state-owned financial institutions that then continued the soft budget for public enterprises, removing incentives for their reform or sale. It is regrettably clear that many governments postpone fundamental reform, especially about

BOX 3.7 (continued)

risen from less than CFAF 90 billion to CFAF 112 billion. In 1991, CIE posted its first profit of CFAF 1.2 billion, and profits have since grown steadily.

The government has already sold half its 49 percent share to 4,000 small investors through a public offering on the Abidjan bourse.

Winners. All stakeholders have benefited from private participation in the sector. Shareholders have received dividends of 10 percent each year. The government can now focus on sectoral policy and regulation. It no longer provides cash injections and other subsidies, and it receives all revenues (net of lease fees and the cost of fuel and energy purchases), plus corporate taxes and dividends. Current tariffs are high enough to ensure the sector's financial equilibrium, with self-financing ratios of about 25 percent.

Employees have also fared well, receiving a 5 percent stake in the company under advantageous terms, a 2 percent wage increase in 1994, and generous benefits by local standards. More than half the employees have also received on-the-job training. Compulsory layoffs have been avoided with staff reductions limited to natural attrition and firings limited to cases of malfeasance. Consumers also are better off. Tariffs have fallen in real terms, and in the wake of the devaluation, lifeline rates for low-income families were introduced.

The future. Capitalizing on the recent discovery of oil and natural gas, the government negotiated an independent power project with private investors. Construction of the gas-fired 100 megawatts unit is near completion, with negotiations for an additional 65 megawatts of capacity already under way. While much remains to be done to secure a competitive and efficient power sector, early experience with private participation has produced substantial benefits and convinced the government to redouble efforts to encourage more private investment.

---

an issue as sensitive as privatization, until a crisis or near-crisis stage is reached—that is, until their backs are against the wall.

Donors thus have to be selective in their assistance, expending greater effort in assessing whether country conditions—and commitment—are suitable for carrying out the policies and projects recommended. Donors must recognize that there are few technical solutions to what are basically political problems and that the commitment to cut off credits to nonviable public enterprises, to establish biting fiscal controls, and to impose macroeconomic stability must come from within. Donor coordination in this fashion was particularly effective in Zambia.

For tradable goods, the first lesson for donors is to create no new public enterprises and to expand no old public enterprises—a lesson largely learned. Almost no donor today lends or offers grants to create a purely public enterprise,

BOX 3.8 PRIVATIZATION OF ENTERPRISE GOVERNANCE IN THE KYRGYZ REPUBLIC

The government of the Kyrgyz Republic has demonstrated its eagerness to privatize most state enterprises rapidly. State ownership will nonetheless remain significant for a period of time, including utilities excluded from the privatization program; shares retained by the State Property Fund (SPF) in partly privatized enterprises, pending their disposal through cash and voucher auctions; and shares in enterprises included in the next two years' privatization program but not yet privatized.

The SPF is responsible for managing the state's ownership interest in the last two categories of enterprises. But it has not effectively exercised its responsibility—in part because of the institution's lack of expertise, coupled with its legitimate focus on implementation of the privatization program, and in part because of the lack of appropriate information, reporting, and control instruments. As a result, the SPF gave up its portfolio management responsibility in some key sectors to line ministries or to state holding companies (thus recreating the old dependence of enterprises on the state). In other sectors, the SPF's supervision has been little more than formal, and the accountability of managers to shareholders, including the state, has been minimal or nonexistent.

To overcome these problems, the SPF is appointing independent private financial and management experts to act as fiduciaries on its behalf, as owner. The experts will be selected in a transparent manner on the basis of their expertise and experience in management. They will be appointed on a one-year renewable contract and compensated according to their performance, including payment in enterprise shares held by the SPF. The SPF intends to implement this approach in 1995 in about 20 enterprises distributed across various sectors in which the state still holds 50 percent or more of the equity. If the experiment succeeds, it will be extended widely.

This approach has several important merits. First, by privatizing the corporate governance function, it promotes the use of market mechanisms and is thus consistent with the current reform philosophy of the government. Second, it places responsibility for governance in the hands of skilled resources. Indeed, while the enterprises' managers and the line ministries have considerable engineering and technical skills, they generally lack entrepreneurial, financial, and market management expertise and orientation. Third, it avoids the creation in the SPF (or elsewhere in the government) of a large civil service—to deal with a mostly temporary issue, the full and rapid privatization of all but a limited number of enterprises.

at least one designed to produce a tradable good. Some low-income countries are still creating public enterprises, but without donor aid and usually contrary to donor advice. Better use of the public expenditure review exercise is required to consolidate this viewpoint of what constitutes priority actions.

The second lesson: the legitimate donor operations for industrial public enterprises are those that assist in the reform and privatization processes. These involve "passive" restructuring—preparing the firm for sale, dealing with excess labor, cleaning up the balance sheet, determining environmental liabilities, and assisting in the attraction of stable, competent private managers, lessors, and purchasers.

For public enterprises in infrastructure, the situation is much more complex and the recommended actions more nuanced. The objective is clear: to create an environment in which infrastructure firms can attract private financing, management, and ownership, while protecting social welfare. But given typical country and market conditions, donors are likely first to have to assist in removing major distortions in pricing, correcting regulatory deficiencies, and enhancing competition in and contestability of markets. And while these reforms are being constructed, direct long-term financing of infrastructure firms, by the donors, may be justified—if the country has endorsed a sound policy approach, and agrees with the goal of moving to greater private sector involvement.

In more advanced countries, donors should examine the prospects for immediate involvement of the private sector as manager or financier of the infrastructure firm in question. And it is even possible that partial or full private ownership of the enterprise might be the optimal course of action. Even when the latter actions are preferred, donors retain a substantial role: as facilitators of the process, as providers of technical assistance, as lenders for investment and financing (though more and more rarely), and as guarantors of private loans and equity investments.

Donors must also redouble their efforts to help governments remove subsidies (box 3.9), retrench labor (box 3.10), rationalize tariff regimes, create good regulatory systems, and unbundle integrated firms and networks into smaller, more manageable, more accountable units. In particular, donors must help governments bring public enterprise finances out of the dark and shed light on the complete flow of funds between government and public enterprises— to reveal the real gains and losses of the sector and the cost of inaction, in terms of forgone job opportunities. For example, a 1994 audit of public enterprise performance in Uganda showed that in the 1990s direct and indirect subsidies to public enterprises have averaged $180 million a year, five times the spending on health. The return flow from the enterprises to the government has been very small. The sum transferred is equal to about $6,000 per state enterprise employee per year, over and above the wage and salaries bill. Alarmed by these numbers, the country's leaders immediately stepped up the pace and scope of reform.

Only when armed with such information can decisionmakers and the public assess the real costs of performance and the opportunities forgone. And only then can public enterprise managers be judged. Otherwise, poor performance

BOX 3.9 WHO BENEFITS FROM PUBLIC ENTERPRISE SUBSIDIES?

The professed rationale for subsidized provision of goods and services by public enterprises is to help the poor. In practice, the benefits of such subsidies rarely reach the poor. Indeed, the poor often bear the burden of financing the subsidies. All too often, the poor either consume very little of the goods or services being subsidized, or intermediaries reap much of the premium created by subsidies.

A recent survey of electricity consumption in the urban areas of several low-income countries shows that the poorest income groups have little access to electricity. In Lusaka, Zambia, only 28 percent of households in the poorest income quintile had access to electricity compared with 70 percent for the richest quintile. In Praia, Cape Verde, while 82 percent of the richest quintile enjoyed access, less than half of the poorest quintile did. Even where the poor have access, they consume far less electricity than do the rich. In Manila, Philippines, nine of ten households in the poorest quintile had access to electricity, but their per capita consumption was only 77 Kwh/month— 17 percent of the consumption of the richest quintile. The benefits to the poor from subsidizing electricity are marginal. They would be better off if subsidies were reduced and the resulting increase in investable funds used to expand access.

In Mauritania, richer households have access to subsidized piped water provided by the public water authority. The poor get their supplies from itinerant water-sellers, who obtain water from public enterprises at subsidized rates, and then charge poor customers several times those rates. In Tanzania, it has been estimated that the poorest fifth of the population receives only about 10 percent of government subsidies for water, whereas the richest fifth receives about 40 percent.

In manufacturing as well, subsidies usually do not benefit the poor. In Bangladesh, the publicly owned sugar and cotton spinning mills had poor financial results for many years. Subsidized provision of the goods produced was a major cause of this. The poor did not benefit because sugar is consumed mainly by richer urban households and poor households rely on sugar substitutes. Yarn was indeed consumed by poor weavers, but the price they paid was substantially higher than the factory prices. The difference went to marketing intermediaries, who took advantage of excess demand to jack up retail prices. The publicly owned jute industry frequently tried to subsidize jute farmers by buying raw jute at much-above market prices, incurring huge losses in the process. Farmers did not necessarily get the higher prices. Benefits were reaped instead by dishonest enterprise staff colluding with marketing intermediaries.

BOX 3.10 WHAT ABOUT LABOR? CREATE RATHER THAN PRESERVE JOBS

The fear of adding to unemployment is one of the biggest obstacles to privatization of any sort. Four encouraging observations:

First, and critical, private investment in most low-income countries creates more jobs than public investment. Governments in these settings would do better to concentrate on job creation through private initiative rather than job preservation in less efficient areas.

Second, the incidence of increased unemployment as a direct result of privatization is lower than anticipated. Some countries have started their privatization programs with companies that were in good condition and not overstaffed (in Morocco, for example) or where the new owners immediately invested and actually hired new workers (telecommunications in several countries). In other countries (Bangladesh, Malaysia, Tunisia, Venezuela, and elsewhere), policy-makers have issued instructions to selling agents and buyers that no layoffs would be allowed for a certain period after sale.

Third, where layoffs have been sizable, they almost always have been "sweetened" by generous severance packages, with terms greatly exceeding the existing labor laws (in Argentina and Pakistan, for example).

Fourth, labor can be persuaded that the privatization process is beneficial by means other than cash payments. Many countries give shares, or sell them at a low price, to workers. In Russia, workers and managers in enterprises obtained at least 25 percent and often 51 percent of the shares before voucher auctions. In Egypt, one firm being privatized solved the problem of excess labor by offering parcels of farmland to those who departed voluntarily. The demand far outstripped the supply.

---

will continue to be attributed to the costs of meeting noncommercial goals and strategic objectives.

To repeat, none of this will be easy. Scant human resource bases and weak institutional systems—common problems in low-income countries, and ones that are not capable of overnight resolution—will impede the adoption of the proposed approach. And one must not underestimate the political obstacles to fundamental reform of public enterprises. Fears of increased unemployment, foreign ownership, concentrated wealth, and lost patronage and perks—all constitute powerful barriers to change. Many thus conclude that gradualism is the more realistic strategy, and that optimal donor efforts are those devoted to education, training, and institution-building—actions that, it is hoped, lay the base for progressive change in the longer term.

While not disputing the severity of the impediments, three concluding observations that question the gradualist perspective are in order:

- First, regarding public enterprise reform, gradualism is exactly what has been tried, and found wanting, in the vast majority of low-income countries over the past 15 years. A recommendation for gradualism is, in many low-income countries, an acknowledgment that the losses and the missed opportunities will continue indefinitely. One must aspire to action of a more immediate impact than can be expected from training or educational programs.

- Second, the proposed strategy—moving farther and faster with private involvement in public enterprises, and concentrating efforts on the largest firms—is actually quite sparing of institutions and administrators in low-income countries, as it reduces demands on government to monitor and manage productive activities and stimulates the growth of the indigenous private sector.

- Third, the political sensitivities are many and real, but reforms in industrial and middle-income countries have generated great public support by calling attention to the high costs and low quality of public enterprise goods and services. Some bold leaders in low-income countries have embarked on this path—and more can be expected to follow.

CHAPTER 4

Building robust financial systems— difficult but pressing

AN efficient and vibrant financial system contributes much to economic development. It mobilizes savings and allocates them to investments by private entrepreneurs. It also screens borrowers, manages risks, and operates the payment and settlement systems. And it ensures that dynamic parts of the economy are well funded. Getting financial systems in low-income countries from where they are to where they should be will not be easy, because financial reforms are among the most difficult to formulate and implement.

Financial reforms must begin by stopping the hemorrhaging of state enterprises that lies at the root of the fiscal deficit and the problems of the banking system. State enterprises account for a good part of the assets of public sector–dominated banking systems in low-income countries, and many of these loans are nonperforming. Such loans are a major drain on the banking systems, which are unable to enforce financial discipline on either state enterprises or privileged borrowers. The state enterprises must be liquidated or privatized into a competitive environment. Only then can the banking system be improved. Similarly, a major effort has to be made to privatize the banks. Since this is likely to be difficult and time-consuming, it is best done in conjunction with promoting new entry—the diversification of institutions, mechanisms, and instruments is a prerequisite to competition and to lasting financial deepening. Also needed is a major effort to strengthen prudential regulation and supervision, enhance and multiply information flows, and strengthen accounting and auditing standards. This in turn requires training—to create the critical mass of human resources to strengthen the financial system.

India, Pakistan, and Sri Lanka are making good progress toward building solid financial systems. This has been spurred by the development of a vibrant private sector, the inflow of foreign direct investment, and expanded trade opportunities. And this has attracted new banks and nonbank financial institutions that compete with public sector banks and take market share away from them. Such developments underscore the importance of creating an environment that fosters the growth of strong and creditworthy borrowers—a precondition for a robust and competitive financial system.

Financial reforms must stop the hemorrhaging
of state enterprises that lies at the root
of the fiscal deficit and the problems of the banking system

Despite some progress, financial systems remain weak in Sub-Saharan Africa, Bangladesh, and economies in transition. Broad money as a percentage of GDP is often used as a measure of financial deepening. In Sub-Saharan Africa, broad money averages between 20 and 25 percent of GDP, compared with 40 percent in Pakistan, 60 percent in India, and 80 percent in China. Even in oil-rich Nigeria, it has been as low as 18 percent of GDP, and in Ghana, despite a decade of macroeconomic adjustment, 17 percent of GDP. These countries must accelerate difficult structural and institutional reforms in the financial sector if their private sectors are to develop.

What went wrong?

Interventionist policies of the past crippled the fledgling financial systems of many low-income countries, including most of those in Sub-Saharan Africa. Large budget deficits were monetized, and inflation followed. To keep nominal rates from rising, interest rates were controlled. But the resulting reduction in real rates reduced incentives for the formal banking system to intermediate savings. It also fostered capital flight and encouraged enterprises with access to credit to overborrow. Inefficient public enterprises grew at the expense of the more efficient private sector. Many commercial banks were nationalized. Credit was allocated by government decree. And banks lost their ability to screen and assess credit risks. Central banking and oversight withered to the detriment of the banking system. Bad loans accumulated, and the losses were periodically recognized and monetized—adding to the bouts of inflation and the unpredictability of the economic environment. This situation has left most low-income countries ill-equipped to generate the private supply response to structural reforms.

What has been done?

During the past few years several low-income countries have begun the difficult and laborious task of reform. Economic stabilization has lowered budget deficits, reduced inflation, and restored trade by bringing the exchange rate toward market clearing levels. There has been important progress in financial sector policies, infrastructure, and institutions. And IDA has been quite active in supporting these reforms (box 4.1)

India, Pakistan, and Sri Lanka reduced state intervention in the financial sector, liberalized interest rates, removed credit ceilings, and allowed some entry by local and foreign banks—though still in a restricted fashion. These countries also restructured insolvent banks, privatized some banks, put into place prudential lending and capital adequacy guidelines accompanied by better supervision, and made major strides in developing their capital markets to attract or accommodate large inflows of foreign portfolio investment. New banks have entered the markets in India (box 4.2) and Pakistan to cater to the large increase in business activity, and total or partial privatizations of public banks are showing positive results.

Bangladesh also has liberalized interest rates and eliminated directed credit except for a small amount for export and small industry. But even with the denationalization of two banks and the entry of new local foreign banks, public sector banks account for 60 percent of the banking system, and nonperforming loans account for more than two-thirds of their assets.

In China, despite recent progress, the banking system remains highly segmented and fragmented. State banks, which still dominate the system, lend mostly to state-owned enterprises with a large portfolio of nonperforming assets at controlled interest rates. Rural and urban cooperatives, which are less controlled and regulated, lend to collectively owned enterprises. And foreign and joint venture banks service joint ventures and foreign firms. Prudential regulations are slowly replacing economic regulations, but information and skills are limited, and a major reform effort will be required to supervise the myriad financial institutions in this rapidly changing environment (box 4.3).

Sub-Saharan Africa has also made major reform efforts (table 4.1). By the end of 1993, interest rates had been freed (in 27 of the 34 Sub-Saharan countries), credit ceilings eliminated (in 23), directed credit reduced (in 27), prudential lending and capital adequacy guidelines introduced, with greater monitoring and enforcement powers for supervisory agencies (in 21), central banks strengthened (in 21), and money markets activated (in 15). New banking laws have been enacted to strengthen the banking system and protect users (for example, bank secrecy). Banks have also been recapitalized and restructured,

BOX 4.1 IDA INVOLVEMENT IN THE FINANCIAL SECTOR: BALANCING SYSTEMIC REFORM WITH FINANCIAL INTERMEDIATION LENDING

IDA has supported financial sector reforms designed to reduce financial repression, strengthen supervisory and regulatory frameworks, restructure and recapitalize distressed financial institutions, and increase competition and efficiency in the financial system. IDA has also been increasingly active in supporting the development of non-bank financial institutions and capital markets.

At the policy level, as part of an overall macroeconomic stabilization program, reforms have sought to liberalize interest rates, phase out sectoral allocation of credit, reduce implicit and explicit taxation on financial institutions, and phase in indirect monetary control procedures. Such measures have been important components of lending operations in countries such as Bangladesh, Côte d'Ivoire, Ghana, Kenya, Pakistan, Tanzania, and Uganda.

In such low-income countries as Bangladesh, Egypt, Ghana, Guinea-Bissau, Malawi, Mauritius, Pakistan, and Uganda, lending operations in the financial sector have also focused on improving the supervisory and regulatory framework. Banking laws have been revised to strengthen supervisory and regulatory powers of central banks and introduce internationally acceptable prudential lending and capital adequacy standards. Technical assistance programs and twinning arrangements have been used to strengthen off-site and on-site supervision systems and to train bank examiners and supervisors, as well as to improve accounting and auditing capabilities.

At the financial intermediary level in such countries as Bangladesh, Côte d'Ivoire, Ghana, Kenya, Mauritania, Tanzania, and Uganda, financial and technical assistance has been provided for restructuring and recapitalizing financial institutions. In many instances, nonperforming loans of banks have been transferred to special debt collection and restructuring agencies and replaced by government obligations. Accompanying these measures have been privatization programs and reform of bank licensing policies that encourage entry by well-capitalized and reputable banks, legislation allowing entry and operations by nonbank financial institutions, reform of debt recovery procedures, and training programs for strengthening banking skills and know-how.

Between fiscal 1988 and 1995, IDA support for financial sector reforms amounted to about $3.9 billion. About 55 percent of the support was provided under Structural Adjustment Credits, and the balance was through Technical Assistance Projects and Financial Intermediation Credits that are being extended at market rates, in a competitive manner, and through qualified financial institutions that meet prudential capital adequacy ratios and lending criteria. Low-income countries in Africa accounted for about 65 percent of the adjustment operations.

The sector. Publicly owned banks, comprising the State Bank Group and 19 banks nationalized in 1969 and 1980, dominate India's commercial banking system. Privately owned banks and branches of foreign banks account for a little more than 10 percent of assets (totaling about $110 billion) and deposits. Following nationalization, the government instructed publicly owned banks to pursue social and developmental goals. During the 1970s and 1980s, these activities—combined with high operating costs, obsolescent technology (bank labor unions opposed computerization), interest controls, high reserve requirements, directed credit, forced investments in government securities, and loan forgiveness—eroded the effectiveness and performance of these institutions.

India has four "All-India" developmental lending institutions, three of which are majority-owned by the government (with about $17 billion in assets), and several other development institutions specialized for such sectors as agriculture, small industry, and housing. There also are more than 30,000 nonbank financial institutions, most privately owned, and a large number of credit cooperatives. India has one of the world's largest capital markets, featuring capitalization exceeding $100 billion and more than 6,000 listed companies.

Reforming the banks. Indian commercial banking is now undergoing thorough reform. Policy changes since 1991 have included the introduction of tighter asset classification, income recognition, and disclosure norms. Reserve requirements and forced investments are being scaled back. And interest rates are being rationalized and liberalized. The minimum lending rate was removed in October 1994, and the government plans eventually to remove a deposit rate ceiling (currently above market levels).

The government hopes to transform the publicly owned banks from bureaucratic entities into vigorous commercial enterprises. These institutions are now engaged in far-reaching reform, including recapitalization, the introduction of modern computer-based technology, organizational streamlining, and the recovery of nonperforming loans. Over the next few years, the government intends to increase nongovernment equity in the banks to as much as 49 percent (of total equity) and to increase private sector representation on bank boards accordingly.

To improve competition, the Reserve Bank of India (RBI) has authorized several new, well-capitalized private banks and branches of some foreign banks to enter the market, although it continues to restrict entry generally. A functionally autonomous Board of Financial Supervision was established in late 1994 within the RBI, now responsible for commercial banks, development finance institutions, and nonbank financial institutions. The RBI now has a program to upgrade its supervision capabilities.

continued on next page

BOX 4.2 (continued)

Public securities markets. The RBI has begun to develop and deepen India's markets for public securities. This should enable India's various governmental entities to meet their financing needs more efficiently. For the past two years, the RBI has steadily increased its reliance on open-market operations rather than direct controls for monetary management. Under a 1994 RBI-Finance Ministry accord, the Treasury's access to direct RBI financing is to be phased out.

Strengthening capital markets. Liberalized regulation has improved the functioning of India's capital markets. In 1992, the Controller of Capital Issues, which set the pricing of new equity issues, was abolished. The Securities and Exchange Board (SEBI), established in 1988, now reviews the pricing of initial share offerings. The SEBI has acted vigorously to modernize outmoded practices in India's equity markets but has generally set a more liberal approach to market regulation. Twenty-two new private sector mutual funds now compete with funds offered by the government-owned Unit Trust of India. Overseas investors have placed a large volume of funds in India's equity markets since they were liberalized in late 1992. Equity trading has strained the capacity of the existing transactions and custody system, and the authorities have acted rapidly to help ease regulations and practices designed for a smaller system.

BOX 4.3 CHINA: THE MAKING OF A FINANCIAL SYSTEM

The development of China's financial sector has lagged behind that of its fast-growing real sector. Until fairly recently the financial sector consisted only of four specialized banks (the Agricultural Bank, the Bank of China, the Industry and Commercial Bank, and the People's Construction Bank). Today a vast network of rural and urban cooperatives and several hundred nonbank financial intermediaries—trust and investment companies, finance companies, leasing companies, and security corporations—compete with these state banks. Shanghai and Shenzhen have had stock exchanges since 1990, and stock markets are now flourishing in scores of Chinese cities.

Low inflation throughout the 1980s and moderate interest rates (which on average provided savers with zero or positive real returns) stimulated resource mobilization. But with increasing inflation during the past few years, real interest rates on deposits and loans from state banks have turned negative. This has contributed to the rise of smaller, unregulated intermediaries, which are less subject to control and are sometimes owned by the larger banks, to service the township and

BOX 4.3 (continued)

village enterprises and private companies. In many cases, collective and private enterprises are paying relatively high rates of interest to offset the low rates paid by the state enterprises. Large deposits now flow between the formal and informal system depending on the changing relationship between savings and credit interest rates.

Despite efforts to strengthen the central bank—the People's Bank of China (PBC)—prudential regulation and supervision is still embryonic, particularly for specialized banks and small intermediaries that finance collective and private enterprises alike. The decentralization of government under way in China means that control of many state-owned enterprises, which account for 45 percent of China's output, has been transferred to local governments, which influence provincial branches of the PBC. Although one-third to one-half of all large and medium-size state-owned enterprises run at a loss, provincial branches of the PBC have enabled them to fund large investments, which accounts for the fact that large non-performing loans are now estimated to account for 15–20 percent of China's bank assets.

To strengthen the country's segmented financial system, the government is considering a new central banking law under which the PBC would be charged with carrying out an independent monetary policy to maintain a stable value of the currency, replacing direct instruments (such

as credit plans) by indirect ones (such as interest rates and open-market operations), transforming the four big specialized banks obligated to finance state-owned enterprises into commercial banks, and setting up three additional banks for infrastructure, agriculture, and international trade to take over the responsibility for policy lending. The PBC would be overseen by the proposed state monetary policy committee, which would be chaired by the PBC governor and include several cabinet ministers.

The World Bank has supported China's efforts to develop its financial sector since the late 1980s. Specialized institutions were equipped to appraise borrowers and manage international loans (such as projects sponsored by the Bank together with the China Investment Bank). Major programs currently being implemented or designed include components to:

■ Advise on major policy issues (interest rate policies, directed credit, financial sector legislation, and prudential regulations).
■ Help develop monetary policy instruments and practices.
■ Design and automate a nationwide payment system.
■ Develop supervisory, regulatory, research, and fiscal agent skills within the central bank.
■ Train bank staff in accounting and audit standards and functions.
■ Develop rules needed to regulate capital markets.

TABLE 4.1 BANK REFORMERS IN SUB-SAHARAN AFRICA

Liberalization and/or rationalization of interest rates	Restructuring of banks	Privatization of banks	Liquidation of banks
Benin	Cameroon	Cameroon	Benin
Burundi	Côte d'Ivoire	Côte d'Ivoire	Côte d'Ivoire
Congo	Ghana	Guinea-Bissau	Guinea
Côte d'Ivoire	Guinea	Madagascar	Niger
The Gambia	Kenya	Mauritania	Rwanda
Ghana	Madagascar	Senegal	Senegal
Kenya	Mali		
Madagascar	Mauritania		
Malawi	Rwanda		
Mauritania	Senegal		
Mozambique	Tanzania		
Rwanda	Uganda		

Note: This table does not comprehensively list all the financial sector reforms undertaken.
Source: World Bank 1994.

liquidated, or privatized in about 25 countries (table 4.2). The number of government-owned and controlled banks was reduced from 140 in the late 1980s to about 115 in 1993. During the same period, the number of private banks rose from 80 to 115, and their share in the assets of the banking system increased from 30 percent to more than 40 percent.

Despite these major improvements, important structural weaknesses remain in low-income countries. Banks continue to finance central government deficits and overextended and uneconomical public enterprises. Typically, about 40 percent of domestic credit (and sometimes as much as 80 percent) goes to the public sector. Credit in the private sector—when it is not crowded out—is garnered by large and politically well-connected firms and traders. Most farmers and small and medium-size indigenous firms have little access to credit, and their growth is limited to what they can finance from retained earnings.

Government-owned or controlled banks still dominate in many low-income countries. In Sub-Saharan countries, they account for more than half the banking system. In most cases, they have weak management, limited banking skills, and ineffective internal controls, and their balance sheets do not reflect their precarious financial position. Credit evaluation of state enterprises is virtually nonexistent because the public banks generally allocate credit following directives from the government—despite the official elimination of directed credit. These loans have the explicit or implicit backing of the government, so banks seldom evaluate the creditworthiness of public sector borrowers.

TABLE 4.2 PROGRESS IN THE FINANCIAL SECTOR
IN SUB-SAHARAN AFRICA

Notable progress	Progress	Slight progress	Regressing or repressed financial system
Botswana	Benin	Burkina Faso	Burundi
The Gambia	Côte d'Ivoire	Gabon	Cameroon
Lesotho	Eritrea	Guinea	Central African Republic
Mauritius	Ghana	Guinea-Bissau	Chad
Uganda	Madagascar	Kenya	Congo
	Malawi	Mali	Ethiopia
	Mauritania	Sierra Leone	Mozambique
	Namibia	Swaziland	Niger
	Senegal	Zambia	Nigeria
		Zimbabwe	Tanzania
			Togo

Influential private firms often continue to borrow without adequate scrutiny from either affiliated private banks or public banks. Prudential regulation and supervision remain inadequate, and bank insolvency is not quickly detected. Even when it is detected, governments often are reluctant to close banks because of the adverse impact on economic activity and because they are financially unable to meet calls on explicitly or implicitly insured deposits.

Governments in many countries continue to restructure problem banks by periodically swapping nonperforming loans with government and central bank obligations. But bank recapitalization alone is ineffective because it has to be repeated if the underlying causes are not addressed. The costs have been enormous: typically 7–10 percent of GDP spread over four to ten years. With the government absorbing these losses, there naturally is the expectation that it will do so again, leading to continued losses by poorly supervised banks. So crises recur, as in Mauritania and particularly Tanzania, where public sector bank recapitalization in 1991 is estimated to have cost about 20 percent of GDP. Despite this costly recapitalization, 70 percent of the assets of the National Bank of Commerce, the main public sector bank with 82 percent of the system's assets, are nonperforming; and a serious collection effort has yet to start.

Governments typically finance these large losses by issuing bonds, and interest on the bonds affects the budget for years to come, at an annual cost often equal to total government spending on health. Add to these interest costs direct government expenditures on public enterprises (5–7 percent of GDP) and treasury obligations to service public enterprise debts, and the burden of public enterprises (as noted in chapter 3) rockets to a staggering 8–12 percent of GDP.

The point is that a large part of these losses is hidden in the banking system—exposed only periodically when a banking crisis threatens. Then, governments often resort to a bout of inflation, possibly adding to economic uncertainty and dampening savings, private investment, and growth. The burden is particularly harsh for small-scale farmers and entrepreneurs denied credit. Unless the dominant position of public enterprises is reduced and their privileged access to bank credit is stopped, economic stability is threatened—and the banking system faces ruin.

What remains to be done?

The development of a robust banking system in low-income countries will require that countries address the underlying weakness of the system—not the symptoms. This is a long and arduous process that requires consistent actions on many fronts to complement the effort on the fiscal front. For Sub-Saharan countries that means building a sound and efficient payment system (in many countries, it still takes two to three weeks to clear a check). It also means restoring the safety and soundness of the financial system (banking and nonbanking), which at a minimum provides basic banking services, particularly trade finance, to a broad segment of the population and firms. And it means introducing better accounting, legal, and supervisory systems and a major effort to upgrade skills at all levels. In Asian economies, it means continuing to restructure and privatize public banks, opening them to competition from the private sector, strengthening prudential regulation and supervision, and developing capital and money markets.

Sever the link between banks and loss-makers

In most countries, the most difficult challenge is to sever the link between nonperforming public enterprises and state banks by cutting the enterprises off from new credit and collecting outstanding loans. It has proved difficult, if not impossible, for state banks to enforce a hard budget constraint on these enterprises. State banks not only roll over loans to public enterprises as they come due, they even increase their exposure—often through the capitalization of unpaid interest. When central banks attempt to enforce credit ceilings, enterprises often build up large intercompany arrears, including those to private firms. As these arrears accumulate and threaten the solvency of banks and enterprises, the central bank is forced to relax credit again.

These failings are especially severe for large public utilities and heavy industries. Although among the most inefficient and financially strapped enterprises (often because they sell their products or services at subsidized prices, and often to public entities that do not pay their bills), they are not allowed to close because they provide essential or strategic services. At best, hard budget constraints can be effectively imposed only on private firms or small public enterprises—and these are already starved for capital and prime candidates for liquidation or privatization. The result is that state banks continue to accumulate large losses and require frequent recapitalization. The drain of big enterprises is likely to worsen as they face increased competition from imports and domestic private producers. That is why it is so urgent to privatize these enterprises and to use the proceeds to reduce high-cost government debt that crowds out the private sector and increases real interest rates. The proceeds could also be used to restore the integrity of the contractual savings systems that governments have often used to finance their deficits. But governments will be persuaded to act on these difficult issues only when the true costs of recapitalization and inaction—in terms of money and lost job opportunities—are made transparent.

Go beyond recapitalization

One of the main reasons restructuring of banking systems has often failed is that governments normally have borne the entire cost and have not changed the incentives facing the banks and their managers. Restructuring has not extended to banks' incentives system or the structure of the banking sector. Losses have seldom been shared with other stakeholders (borrowers, depositors, shareholders, and managers) or accompanied by vigorous loan recovery efforts. In most cases, restructuring has merely transferred nonperforming

> *One of the main reasons restructuring of banking systems has often failed is that governments normally have borne the entire cost and not changed the incentives facing the banks and their managers*

loans to loan recovery agencies, where they languish uncollected. Loans went from being undermanaged in the banks to unmanaged in these agencies. In Ghana, less than 20 percent of debt was recovered, and in Cameroon and Tanzania, less than 5 percent. In Kenya, the new bank established to take over the bad loan portfolio of commercial banks has itself become financially distressed—because it was forced to lend to troubled state enterprises rather than pursue delinquent borrowers. In contrast, Chile's successful bank restructuring of 1986 required the banks, under new ownership and management, to use a large share of their profits to repurchase nonperforming assets from the central bank, where they had been placed in special accounts. This gave the banks the incentive and the breathing space to work with their clients to maximize loan recovery.

In general, bank restructuring is extremely difficult and demanding, especially in countries where legal and management skills are in short supply and where the private sector lacks the means to buy the companies or their assets. This is particularly the case in Eastern Europe, where cutting off credits to public enterprises imposes, at least in the short run, unacceptably high costs on the economy through the loss of productive capacity and sharp rises in unemployment. In this case, what is needed is Chapter 11–type bankruptcy proceedings, which allow for a temporary moratorium on enforcement of creditors' claims, to permit an examination of the feasibility of a reorganization, and during which banks continue to lend to the enterprise so it can function during the reorganization. The challenge, of course, is to prevent the moratorium from delaying the reform process. One such approach is being implemented by the Kyrgyz Republic. It has established a solvency resolution scheme where the government budget, and not commercial banks, will provide, in a transparent manner, the financial resources required by public enterprises to support the cost of care and maintenance, orderly liquidation (in particular, funding of severance payments), or passive restructuring. At the end of the process, nonviable enterprises will have been liquidated, and successfully restructured enterprises will resume normal relations with the banking system on commercial terms and be offered up for sale immediately (box 4.4).

Reduce the role of state banks

The lesson for low-income countries is that incentives must change alongside restructuring efforts. And this involves bank privatization and changes in management—since it is much easier to establish an arm's length relationship between properly regulated and supervised private banks and their private clients. In Africa, Guinea-Bissau, Madagascar, Mauritania, and most CFA-zone countries have privatized or liquidated banks as part of bank restructuring, but this has yet to happen in a large number of countries.

In general, liquidation and privatization has proved easier for the small and medium-size banks, particularly when it is part of an overall reform program that allows new entry in the banking system. Pakistan and some CFA countries are examples. In 1990, Pakistan successfully privatized two of the smallest public sector banks—the Muslim Commercial Bank and Allied Bank Limited. Within three years, the banks tripled their deposits and doubled their profits, largely through improved services, cost cutting, and a vigorous collection effort. In 1991, the government allowed private banks to compete with public banks, which were still reeling under the pressure of $2.4 billion in nonperforming loans. Nine new local banks were licensed that year. Foreign banks also have expanded their business: with only 75 of 7,740 branches nationwide they have captured more than a quarter of banking system deposits. The interest rate spread of public sector banks dropped by 33 percent in less than two years because of increased competition.

It should also be stressed that the success of banking reform in Pakistan owes much to general economic policy, which has liberalized the foreign exchange market and trade, privatized large public enterprises, and attracted foreign invest-ment. These measures in turn increased the demand for financial services by a vibrant and increasingly sophisticated and discriminating private sector.

Some countries are adopting a more measured approach in restructuring their banking system. In addition to allowing new entry, they are partially pri-vatizing state banks. India's largest state-owned bank raised $700 million through a public equity issue to 2.3 million investors, augmenting paid-in cap-ital and reducing the central bank's share from 98 percent to 68 percent (expect-

---

BOX 4.4 INSOLVENCY RESOLUTION SCHEME IN THE KYRGYZ REPUBLIC:
A DIFFICULT AND DEMANDING TASK

The Kyrgyz Republic's Enterprise Re-form and Resolution Agency (ERRA) manages the restructuring or liquida-tion of large insolvent state-owned industrial enterprises that cannot be easily privatized, but whose continuing operation compromises the survival of other enterprises and the banks. A list of twenty-nine large enterprises has been drawn up by the government, based on their level of indebtedness to the budget, to the banks, and to other enterprises or creditors, including their own personnel.

ERRA is semiautonomous agency whose primary goal is the closure of unviable entities. Its board of directors is responsible to the government and has sole power and authority to decide on the future of all selected enterprises. ERRA will focus on liqui-dating unviable business units and

disposing of excess or unproductive assets; separating and disposing of peripheral activities, including social assets; eliminating overstaffing; and balance sheet restructuring, including purchase of nonperforming loans from commercial banks against an equivalent reduction of the banks' lia-bilities to the central bank. All ERRA restructuring programs are clearly time-bound. If, at the expiration of an agreed period (12–18 months), a financial turnaround is not evident, the enterprise will be liquidated. The recently approved Bankruptcy Law gives ERRA wide and sufficient pow-ers to liquidate or restructure enter-prises under its responsibility.

All selected enterprises have been cut off from the banking sector to stem the flow of bad loans. Each enterprise has been placed under "care and

continued on next page

BOX 4.4 (continued)

maintenance" to prevent further buildup of inventories and payables, and to minimize costs. Pending completion of a viability study and a decision regarding the enterprise's closure or restructuring, only a core team of personnel is kept at work to ensure that buildings and equipment are kept in good condition. In some instances, a small team of salesmen is organized to sell existing inventory and raise revenues. All other employees are put on administrative leave. Essential social services—chiefly health care, winter heating, and schooling—continue to be provided to all employees and their families during the review period.

The budget, and not commercial banks, will provide financial resources transparently to support the cost of care and maintenance, orderly liquidation (in particular, funding of severance payments), or passive restructuring.

No new capital investments will be funded from government sources. Working capital and financing for maintenance or repair of essential equipment may also be provided to maintain those components of an enterprise with good prospects of viability. At the end of the process, nonviable enterprises will have been liquidated and successfully restructured enterprises will be cut off from further direct or indirect government financial resources. They will resume relations with the banking sector on commercial terms and be offered up for sale immediately.

Performance will be measured by the declining amount of financial transfers from ERRA to the enterprises, either because the enterprise is liquidated and redundancy payments stop after a period of time, or because the company is starting to generate positive cash flows.

ed to fall to 55 percent after a second public offering). This approach will be replicated in other state-owned banks, which are expected to raise private equity capital up to 49 percent of their share capital, with corresponding representation of private shareholders on their boards. The banks are undertaking a major effort to collect on some $12 billion in nonperforming loans (6 percent of GDP and 12 percent of the assets of the banking system), and intend to sell their urban real estate holdings. These measures are intended to reduce government funds needed for recapitalization.

But liquidating or privatizing the state banks that account for the bulk of banking system assets is difficult—both economically and politically. Yet maintaining their dominant position, even while allowing new entry, does little to change their performance, as Tanzania shows. An alternative is to downsize banks as a way of reducing the cost of restructuring and to seek management contracts with reputable domestic and foreign banks, preferably with a preferred equity position, to run the downsized public banks until improvements attract suitable buyers. Furthermore, as is being contemplated in Macedonia and proposed in Tanzania, the government could break the larger state banks into competing networks that service both urban and rural areas—as they were prior to their nationalization in the 1960s and 1970s—and then sell them to reputable private domestic and foreign banks.

But even attracting serious and reputable private banks will be difficult unless the government reduces the dominant position of public enterprises and develops an attractive environment to stimulate the private sector. Indeed, a good part of the development of the banking system in China, India, Pakistan, and Sri Lanka was stimulated by the growth of a competitive pri-

The difficulty of restructuring and privatizing banks and banking systems is often compounded by ethnic considerations, and privatization methods should include ways to broaden ownership structures

vate sector that demanded a wider range of services, delivered in an efficient and cost-effective way. In other words, the privatization of banks has a much better chance of success when it is part of an overall effort to develop competitive markets in which the private sector is given the opportunity to grow. The development of a competitive banking system in turn helps the development of a competitive private sector since borrowers will not be limited to a few banks that service only selected and well-connected clients. The presence of foreign banks has often promoted and facilitated foreign investment from their countries.

In many low-income countries, the difficulty of restructuring and privatizing banks and banking systems is often compounded by ethnic considerations, and privatization methods should include ways to broaden ownership structures.

Privatization has its risks. In some cases, banks have been sold in a nontransparent manner and in an unregulated environment to privileged buyers who used them to finance their own activities. In other cases banks were sold with little information about the quality of the portfolio (box 4.5). Privatization, if it is to succeed, must be done transparently. Banks should be sold only to qualified, reputable buyers who have access to information about the finances of the banks (based on portfolio audits by reputable independent accounting firms). Privatized banks have to be properly regulated and supervised, and should not be bailed out if they fail.

BOX 4.5 HOW NOT TO PRIVATIZE A BANK

Banks in Bangladesh were nationalized at independence from Pakistan, but in the early 1980s two banks were denationalized—both in poor financial condition and overburdened with bad debt from parastatals.

Because financial information was not readily available, potential buyers were provided with little information about portfolio quality. Many investors, however, saw the opportunity to buy a bank as the chance of a lifetime. The value of the bank was therefore fixed by the government, and when portfolio problems were later uncovered, the government refused to adjust the price. It also refused to honor its loan guarantees to these banks, although guarantees to nationalized banks were honored. New owners were not allowed to shut loss-making branches and were required to abide by service and employment rules established in 1982.

As a result, the new owners were not able to recapitalize their banks sufficiently, and both continued to lose money. Worse yet, the public came to mistrust privatization, hampering efforts to privatize other banks.

Balance competition with solvency

Competition and privatization are not an end in themselves. They are a means to improve the quality and reduce the cost of financial services to a broad segment of the population. But a warning is in order: experiments with liberal entry without adequate supervision have failed in Africa. In Nigeria, several poorly managed, undercapitalized banks speculated in the foreign exchange market, and their losses now threaten the deposit insurance institution's solvency.

The challenge is to balance the goal of increasing competition and the need to ensure the solvency of financial institutions. Many low-income countries lack the resources to regulate their banking system. Given the high risks in the economic environment and the weak management and information systems, a system that offers extra cushions against risk is desirable. Governments might consider requiring capital-adequacy ratios well above the recommended 8 percent risk-weighted capital regarded as sound by international standards (or raising liability limits for bank owners) and providing some co-insurance from depositors. Low-income countries could encourage reputable foreign or joint-venture banks to help diversify and deepen their financial systems. Reputable banks, seeking to preserve their reputation, are less likely to operate objectionably even if they cannot be consistently well supervised.

A market-determined interest rate is an integral part of a competitive banking system. But to avoid the detrimental effect of high real interest rates, interest rate liberalization has to be phased in with a macroeconomic stabilization program that reduces fiscal deficits. Also essential is a prudential regulation and supervision system that requires banks to enforce hard budget constraints on their borrowers, improve the quality of their portfolio, and improve their capital structure.

Better supervision and prudential regulations. Most countries have strengthened laws and regulations, and some have improved their supervisory and enforcement powers. Indeed, IDA has been particularly active in training. But the information and skills needed to apply these standards remain limited. There are few trained banking supervisors, accountants, and auditors—and off-site and on-site inspection is ineffective. Many countries lack basic accounting and auditing standards, and even where they exist auditors are too pliable. In some West African countries, the banking sector was not covered by a standardized system of accounting and auditing rules until recently. In such cases, neither banking supervisors nor depositors and creditors can detect incipient financial distress.

Because building these skills will be slow, low-income countries should consider twinning or subcontracting arrangements with established foreign institutions such as central banks and qualified accounting firms. A few countries (Bolivia, India, and even Switzerland) are successfully using major accounting firms to supplement their own supervisory authority.

Clear exit procedures, implemented quickly at the point of insolvency. Ultimately, discipline in a competitive banking system comes from the threat of failure. Designing appropriate mechanisms for handling bank crises remains a difficult task, because it requires balancing the objectives of preservation of overall banking stability and the possibility of individual bank failure. Frequently, governments step in to prop up insolvent banks because of the pos-

---

The principal lesson from many countries is that strong professional standards for bank supervision are no substitute for effective political action to deal quickly with insolvent banks

---

sibility of contagion to other institutions, the potential disruption of the payment system, and the state's fiduciary responsibility to depositors as nominal bank supervisor. Bank supervisors become discouraged because of weak political support for their technical recommendations, and a culture of passivity and unprofessionalism seeps into regulatory agencies.

The principal lesson from many countries is that strong professional standards for bank supervision are no substitute for effective political action. Bank closure invariably escalates to the highest political level, particularly in underdeveloped financial systems with a high degree of concentration. Governments that have succeeded in dealing with this difficult problem have typically established, ahead of time, detailed mechanisms and procedures for quickly intervening in insolvent banks in a way that depoliticizes, to the extent possible, the exit process. These measures include replacement of bank management, a vigorous collection effort, sale and disposal of assets, prosecution of fraud, and allocation of losses to shareholders, depositors, and taxpayers—in that order. Quick application of these procedures minimizes chances of contagion to other parts of the financial system and reduces the cost to the government and the risk of recurrence.

Serve small borrowers

Even after the banking system is substantially restructured, small and medium-size enterprises (10–200 employees), microentrepreneurs (fewer than ten employees and including large numbers of the self-employed), and the rural poor are likely to be underserved because of high risk and transaction costs.

Many low-income countries have instituted special programs to provide financial services, particularly credit, to farmers at subsidized rates—often with the support of donor agencies, including IDA. But default rates have been high. Credit intended for the poor often has been preempted by wealthy farmers and well-connected entrepreneurs. Savings mobilization has been poor and transaction costs high. And commercial banks have been reluctant to undertake voluntary lending, while specialized rural financial institutions have not become financially self-sufficient and often have collapsed.

There has been a general failure to establish viable financial intermediaries that can mobilize resources and channel them into productive agricultural and rural enterprises. The same goes for microenterprise programs instituted and managed by governments in urban areas. A recent Bank review of lending of $3.7 billion to small and microenterprises in thirty countries found that performance was best in Latin America, where loans to the individual borrower averaged $22,600 and repayment rates were 92 percent. The worst performance was in Africa, where the average loan was $143,400 and only 62 percent was repaid. Latin America had more competent banks and a more dynamic small business sector—and better program designs.

Small borrowers value safe, reliable, and convenient savings and banking services. Postal savings have been used effectively in many East Asian countries to nurture a savings culture and mobilize rural savings, particularly following reforms that changed the terms of trade in favor of farmers. These systems offer deposit instruments to help with savings and liquidity management, and payments instruments to facilitate small transactions. Similarly, small borrowers value easy access to short-term loans. Such loans and services have been successfully provided by organizations that provide savings and credit at market prices on a permanent basis—instead of short-lived subsidized credit programs, which often fail to reach the intended target group.

Many nongovernmental financial intermediaries and nongovernmental organizations—relying on local savings, careful credit screening, and lending at market rates—have reached a large number of borrowers, particularly women. These organizations reduce default risks significantly through careful selection of borrowers, provision of technical assistance, and prudent use of collateral and joint liability systems. Borrowers open savings accounts, and only those that have repaid earlier small loans are lent larger sums. Such organizations include credit and loan associations, mutual banks in Guinea, Mali, Nigeria, Rwanda, and Zimbabwe, the Grameen Bank in Bangladesh (1.5 million borrowers), BancoSol in Bolivia (40,000 borrowers), BRI Kupides in Indonesia (1.9 million borrowers and 10 million savers), the Kenya Rural Enterprise program (5,000 borrowers), ACCION in Latin America, Women's World Banking in Africa, Asia, and Latin America, and the Fundes Foundation of Switzerland in Latin America.

These institutions have good track records in outreach and enterprise sustainability, two of the most important criteria in microfinance. But their lending is hampered by small capitalization and the high transaction costs associated with providing technical assistance to numerous small borrowers. These organizations need help in the form of seed capital and technical assistance to grow enough to exploit scale economies, evolve into licensed financial institutions (as BancoSol in Bolivia and CorpoSol in Colombia), or have refinancing facilities with banks. Seed capital and technical assistance should, however, be temporary and conditional—first on operational self-sufficiency (revenues covering all nonfinancial costs) and later on full self-sufficiency (no subsidies). Within five to seven years, the better institutions should be able to access capital markets and attract private investors, as some of them are successfully starting to do (box 4.6).

Improve collateral and debt recovery laws

The laws for collateral hamper sound lending and reduce access to credit for many groups. Simple changes in these laws would enable the use of collateral in obtaining credits, a boon to small borrowers (see chapter 2, box 2.4). A related issue is the functioning of the land markets, where better titling registries could improve access to loans. More attention also needs to be paid to expediting debt recovery procedures, which are now slow and cumbersome. Defaulters exploit the protection that laws afford them and creditors are unfairly penalized by the slowness of the court system. As a result, many loans are not forthcoming.

**BOX 4.6 SUCCESSFUL MICROFINANCE INSTITUTIONS:
EMPOWERING THE POOR AND WOMEN**

Recent evaluations of microenterprise programs point to characteristics shared by successful programs and institutions that have reached a large number of poor and female entrepreneurs.

■ Financial services are tailored to the needs of poor entrepreneurs.

■ Operations are streamlined to reduce unit costs.

■ Clients are strongly motivated to repay their loans through the use of group guarantees and other social structures as well as incentives—such as guaranteeing access to repeat loans, increasing loan sizes over time, and offering preferential pricing for those who pay on time.

■ Interest rates and fees reflect the full cost of service delivery.

Some important new small-enterprise initiatives are being developed within the World Bank Group.

IDA has started to work with institutions that have a track record in lending to rural and urban poor microenterprises and operations that are sustainable, replicable, and based on strong savings mobilization. Partnership programs with three nongovernmental organizations (NGOs) were launched to learn more about technical assistance for small and medium-size enterprises and microenterprises. These NGOs are Women's World Banking, Tools for Development of Care (Canada), and Fundes Foundations (Switzerland).

The Bank has allocated $2 million to the Grameen Bank of Bangladesh—a highly successful program that lends primarily to poor women—to assist similar credit programs in other countries. The Bank and a number of donors have launched a Microfinance Program under which the Bank will contribute $30 million over the next three years. Other donors have pledged an additional $170 million through their own programs. The program will provide grants or loans to finance seed capital and technical assistance to institutions devoted to increasing the productive capacity of the very poor. A major purpose is to learn and disseminate the best practices for delivering sustained financial services to the very poor.

The IFC is exploring ways it can assist certain financial intermediaries with access to capital markets and appeal to private investors through its investment in an equity fund that will invest in profitable microfinance institutions in Latin America and in Africa.

Develop nonbank financial institutions and money and capital markets

Alongside the improvement and eventual privatization of banks, the development of nonbank financial institutions and money and capital markets helps deepen financial systems. Pension funds and insurance companies, when properly regulated and managed, could play an increasingly important role in mobilizing savings and financing long-term investment, particularly in infrastructure where earnings are in local currency. Nonbank financial systems have also cropped up in rural areas in many African countries to serve small savers and the informal sector.

Money and capital markets also could get a boost from government obligations. Governments in many low-income countries borrow mostly through the banking system. This makes little sense, for a bank's expertise lies—or should lie—in evaluating credit risk, not simply in investing in government paper, as many banks do. Money and capital markets could help finance the needs of government and those of major infrastructure projects. But developing such markets (and their role in trading securities, enhancing liquidity, and improving firm governance) requires the development of institutions—exchanges, brokers, accountants, rating agencies—and a pool of investors who understand risks and rewards.

Privatization programs that include a large public offer component can help strengthen the banking system by creating a primary and secondary market for corporate securities. The privatization of state-owned enterprises could revive dormant capital markets, as in Argentina, Chile, Malaysia, and Mexico, and more recently in Egypt, Jordan, and Pakistan, and build new ones such as in Mongolia, a small economy in transition (box 4.7). In Ghana, the recent divestiture of minority holdings in several companies more than doubled the market capitalization of the country's stock exchange.

Developing capital markets, instruments, and institutions takes time, but the foundations for this can be laid early. Egypt, Pakistan, and Tanzania have made initial policy reforms to foster capital market development while continuing to place most emphasis on banking reform. This involves technical assistance for legal and regulatory reforms and policy decisions concerning market structure. It is the approach most widely applicable to low-income

---

BOX 4.7 MONGOLIA: USING PRIVATIZATION TO CREATE CAPITAL MARKETS

In 1991, Mongolia decided to privatize 344 large enterprises and 1,601 small businesses through a voucher distribution program. Two types of vouchers were issued: red vouchers for small enterprises and blue vouchers for large firms. Red vouchers were freely tradable, while blue vouchers bought equity shares in large enterprises, which were then freely tradable. A secondary market in red vouchers developed rapidly. In February 1992, the Mongolian stock exchange was opened with an initial offering of large enterprises for vouchers. Within four months, 34 companies were listed on the exchange and 21 companies were fully privatized.

BOX 4.8 IFC: AN INCREASING ROLE IN THE FINANCIAL SECTOR

The IFC has supported financial sector reform in many developing countries. In Africa, it has provided technical assistance, invested in equity, lent money to support operations, promoted the creation of investment funds, helped countries improve their financial sector regulations, and brought much-needed competition and diversity to financial systems dominated by state-owned commercial banks. IFC technical assistance has focused primarily on developing securities markets, building financial institutions, and advising countries about the leasing and regulation of insurance.

In Zambia, the IFC—in collaboration with IDA—spearheaded the creation of the country's first stock exchange, which took just ten months. The IFC has provided advice to The Gambia, Ghana, Kenya, Nigeria, Uganda, and Zimbabwe on development and regulation of money markets, capital markets, and modernization of stock exchange operations. Countries in the CFA zone and Benin and Nigeria have all been assisted in the development of leasing laws. In Kenya, Tanzania, and Uganda, feasibility studies on venture capital funds are being conducted. IFC also has assisted in the review of capital market operations in India, and in China has helped the regulatory commission review new securities regulations.

In most instances, IFC financial loans are African countries' first-ever equity and loan investments. IFC has invested in two money market institutions and a leasing company in Ghana, and has helped the Industrial Bank of Malawi become one of the most successful development institutions in Africa. In Tanzania, IFC investments in a trade finance institution and a leasing company have provided viable alternatives to private borrowers for the first time. In Kenya, the IFC has provided financial assistance to the first private reinsurance company. In Benin and Senegal, the first leasing companies were backed by IFC financial investments. In Asia, where the IFC has been supporting financial intermediaries for a long while, it is now promoting venture capital companies and portfolio investment and management companies.

To facilitate portfolio investments in Africa, the IFC launched the Africa Emerging Markets Fund (AEMF) in 1993, a $30 million, open-ended fund (currently 80 percent invested in 32 stocks in 7 African countries). This fund altered government attitudes toward foreign portfolio investments. As a result of the AEMF example, a number of countries have now liberalized their exchange control regulations to allow freer repatriation of investment earnings and instituted reform measures to reverse past repressive financial sector policies.

The IFC also uses its Emerging Markets Data Base (EMDB) to publicize information on capital markets in developing countries. The EMDB is increasingly used as a benchmark for portfolio managers to gauge performance. Coverage of stocks and countries is constantly increasing: China and Sri Lanka were added in 1993.

countries. The IFC has been particularly active in this area (box 4.8) and the Bank has complemented the IFC's work, especially in policy, institution, and skills development.

The path for reform

Building a robust and competitive financial system is difficult under the best of circumstances. It is particularly difficult and time-consuming when reforming public enterprises and building institutional and regulatory capacity is required not only in the banking system, but also in the legal system. Successful financial reform requires measures on the following fronts:

- Stopping the hemorrhaging of nonperforming enterprises, a major cause of the fiscal deficit and a good part of the assets of the banking system. To the extent possible, these enterprises must be privatized or liquidated (see chapter 3).
- Privatizing the banks themselves and allowing new entry to create a competitive banking system. This is best done as part of an overall program to liberalize the economy.
- Building the financial infrastructure, notably a well-functioning payment and settlement system, prudential regulations and supervision, and the legal infrastructure that allows both borrowers and lenders to enter into flexible and secure transactions that are quickly and efficiently enforced.
- Undertaking a major training program to upgrade skills at all levels in all areas (managers, loan officers, accountants, financial specialists, economists, lawyers, management information specialists, and so on).

The path for reform will vary from country to country, depending on the condition of the banks and the overall market structure, the development of the private sector, the legal framework and institutional capabilities, and the political environment.

Often the most difficult aspect is to cut credit to unviable enterprises and to restructure, liquidate, or privatize the banks. The underlying problem is partly technical but mainly political. The commitment must come from within the country itself.

Until governments generate the consensus for the reform, donors should play a supporting role, not by funding cosmetic balance-sheet restructuring that removes the incentive for reform and aggravates the problem, but by concentrating on laying the groundwork for future reform. This includes backing small, well-designed technical assistance projects that strengthen the legal, accounting, and supervisory frameworks—and providing advice to the government and to key financial institutions.

Statistical appendix

TABLE A1.1 REAL GDP AND PER CAPITA REAL GDP GROWTH
(average annual rates, in percent)

	Real GDP growth			Per capita real GDP growth		
	1981–93	*1981–86*	*1987–93*	*1981–93*	*1981–86*	*1987–93*
Low-income countries	**5.2**	**5.4**	**5.1**	**3.1**	**3.3**	**3.1**
Sub-Saharan Africa	**1.8**	**1.6**	**2.2**	**–1.3**	**–1.5**	**–0.9**
Reforming countries	**2.5**	**0.1**	**4.5**	**–0.7**	**–2.9**	**1.3**
Burundi	4.0	5.0	3.2	1.1	2.1	0.3
Gambia, The	3.8	4.6	3.1	0.1	0.7	–0.5
Ghana	2.8	0.9	4.5	–0.4	–2.4	1.3
Guinea	3.8	..	3.8	0.8	..	0.8
Guinea-Bissau	4.5	4.7	4.4	2.4	3.0	2.0
Kenya	3.3	3.4	3.3	0.0	–0.3	0.2
Madagascar	0.2	–1.0	1.2	–2.7	–3.7	–1.8
Malawi	2.5	1.8	3.1	–0.7	–1.4	–0.2
Mauritania	2.0	1.6	2.2	–0.5	–0.6	–0.5
Mozambique	2.1	–4.4	7.6	–0.5	–6.8	4.9
Nigeria	2.0	–1.7	5.7	–1.2	–4.7	2.2
Sierra Leone	1.3	0.5	2.0	–1.1	–1.8	–0.6
Tanzania	3.5	1.6	5.5	0.5	–1.5	2.5
Uganda	3.5	–1.1	5.5	0.6	–3.1	2.2
Zambia	1.1	0.4	1.7	–2.1	–2.9	–1.4
Zimbabwe	2.7	3.9	1.7	–0.5	0.4	–1.3

(table continues on next page)

TABLE A1.1 (continued)

	Real GDP growth			Per capita real GDP growth		
	1981–93	1981–86	1987–93	1981–93	1981–86	1987–93
Other African countries	**1.1**	**3.0**	**−0.2**	**−1.9**	**−0.1**	**−3.2**
Angola	−0.5	..	−1.0	−3.3	..	−3.8
Benin	3.2	4.3	2.2	0.0	1.1	−0.9
Burkina Faso	3.5	4.8	2.4	0.8	2.2	−0.4
Cameroon[a]	0.8	7.5	−5.0	−2.1	4.6	−7.7
Cape Verde	5.3	6.3	4.4	2.7	3.8	1.8
Central African Republic	0.8	2.2	−0.5	−1.8	−0.4	−3.1
Chad	5.0	7.0	3.4	2.5	4.5	0.8
Comoros	2.5	4.0	1.2	−1.1	0.4	−2.4
Congo[a]	4.2	7.8	1.2	1.0	4.6	−2.0
Côte d'Ivoire	−0.2	1.0	−1.2	−3.9	−2.8	−4.8
Djibouti	0.7	1.8	−0.2	−4.7	−4.5	−4.9
Equatorial Guinea	4.5	..	4.5	2.1	..	2.1
Ethiopia	1.3	1.1	1.6	−1.3	−1.7	−0.9
Lesotho	4.3	1.6	6.7	1.5	−1.3	4.0
Liberia	−1.5	−1.6	..	−4.2	−4.5	..
Mali	2.9	2.7	3.0	0.3	0.4	0.2
Niger	−0.5	−1.4	0.2	−3.7	−4.7	−2.9
Rwanda	1.9	3.4	0.7	−1.0	0.4	−2.1
São Tomé and Principe	0.1	−1.5	1.5	−2.0	−3.3	−1.0
Senegal[a]	2.6	3.3	2.0	−0.3	0.4	−1.0
Somalia	2.0	2.9	0.7	−1.1	−0.2	−2.4
Sudan	2.1	1.6	2.6	−0.6	−1.1	−0.2
Togo	−0.8	0.2	−1.7	−4.1	−2.8	−5.1
Zaire	−0.4	2.3	−2.7	−3.3	−0.9	−5.4
East Asia and the Pacific	**8.0**	**8.1**	**7.9**	**6.6**	**6.7**	**6.5**
China	9.5	9.8	9.3	8.0	8.2	7.8
Other East Asia and the Pacific	**4.1**	**1.8**	**6.2**	**2.2**	**0.7**	**3.7**
Cambodia	6.4	..	6.4	3.0	..	3.0
Kiribati	0.7	0.7	0.7	−1.4	−1.5	−1.4
Lao PDR	4.9	5.0	4.9	2.0	2.1	2.0
Mongolia	..	..	..	..	..	..
Myanmar	2.2	3.9	0.7	0.0	1.7	−1.4

TABLE A1.1 (continued)

	Real GDP growth			Per capita real GDP growth		
	1981–93	*1981–86*	*1987–93*	*1981–93*	*1981–86*	*1987–93*
Solomon Islands	6.6	8.7	4.6	3.4	5.3	1.6
Tonga	1.9	3.7	1.0	2.3	3.7	1.5
Vanuatu	3.1	4.4	1.9	0.7	1.9	−0.4
Viet Nam	4.5	1.0	7.5	2.8	0.3	5.0
Western Samoa	−0.3	0.2	−0.8	−0.7	−0.02	−1.2
South Asia	**5.2**	**5.4**	**5.0**	**2.9**	**3.1**	**2.8**
India	5.1	5.3	5.0	3.0	3.1	2.9
Other South Asia	**5.4**	**5.9**	**4.9**	**2.6**	**3.1**	**2.2**
Afghanistan	..	..	..	..	..	..
Bangladesh	4.5	5.2	4.0	2.2	2.6	1.8
Bhutan	7.4	7.4	7.4	4.4	5.2	3.5
Maldives	7.8	..	8.8	4.7	..	5.4
Nepal	4.8	4.9	4.8	2.2	2.2	2.1
Pakistan	6.0	6.6	5.5	2.8	3.4	2.3
Sri Lanka	4.6	5.4	4.0	3.2	3.8	2.6
Latin America and the Caribbean	**0.7**	**−0.3**	**1.6**	**−1.8**	**−2.8**	**−0.9**
Bolivia[a]	1.0	−1.8	3.5	−1.1	−3.7	1.1
Guyana	−0.8	−2.7	0.8	−1.3	−3.3	0.5
Haiti	−1.5	−0.7	−2.2	−3.3	−2.5	−4.1
Honduras	2.8	1.6	3.9	−0.4	−1.9	0.8
Nicaragua	−0.8	0.2	−1.5	−3.4	−2.6	−4.1
Middle East and North Africa	**..**	**..**	**..**	**..**	**..**	**..**
Egypt, Arab Rep.	4.1	6.3	2.1	1.6	3.6	−0.1
Yemen, Rep.	..	..	..	..	..	..
Eastern and Central Europe	**−4.5**	**3.3**	**−10.7**	**−5.7**	**1.8**	**−11.8**
Albania	−1.0	2.7	−4.1	−2.9	0.6	−5.8
Armenia	−3.4	5.2	−10.8	−4.8	3.6	−12.0
Georgia	−8.2	2.3	−17.3	−8.8	1.5	−17.6
Kyrgyz Republic[a]	0.7	4.0	−2.2	−1.0	2.0	−3.7
Macedonia, FYR[a]	..	..	..	..	..	..
Tajikistan	−2.0	3.6	−6.9	−4.7	0.7	−9.4

a. Lower-middle-income economy but eligible for access to IDA resources.
Source: World Bank data.

TABLE A1.2 SECTORAL GROWTH RATES
(average annual rates, in percent)

	Agriculture		
	1981–93	*1981–86*	*1987–93*
Low-income countries	**3.9**	**4.5**	**3.3**
Sub-Saharan Africa	**1.9**	**1.7**	**1.8**
Reforming countries	**2.5**	**1.5**	**3.2**
Burundi	2.7	4.1	1.5
Gambia, The	4.5	7.4	1.0
Ghana	0.9	−0.2	1.8
Guinea	..	..	3.1
Guinea-Bissau	6.9	8.3	5.8
Kenya	2.2	3.4	1.2
Madagascar	2.1	1.6	2.5
Malawi	3.8	1.6	5.8
Mauritania	2.6	3.0	2.3
Mozambique	2.6	1.8	3.4
Nigeria	2.5	1.2	3.9
Sierra Leone	2.6	1.9	3.4
Tanzania	4.1	3.5	4.8
Uganda	2.8	−1.3	4.5
Zambia	4.0	3.8	4.2
Zimbabwe	0.9	5.3	−3.6
Other African countries	**1.3**	**2.1**	**0.3**
Angola	−0.7	−0.4	−1.2
Benin	4.3	4.7	4.0
Burkina Faso	3.1	5.0	1.4
Cameroon[a]	−0.8	3.6	−4.5
Cape Verde	5.5	4.3	6.6
Central African Republic	1.7	3.0	0.6
Chad	5.1	2.0	8.9
Comoros	2.9	4.1	1.9
Congo[a]	1.8	2.3	1.4
Côte d'Ivoire	0.0	−2.0	1.7
Djibouti	..	−3.4	−1.2
Equatorial Guinea	..	..	−0.7
Ethiopia	1.1	−1.8	3.5
Lesotho	−0.3	0.03	−0.6
Liberia	..	..	..

Industry			Services			Population
1981–93	*1981–86*	*1987–93*	*1981–93*	*1981–86*	*1987–93*	*1981–93*
7.6	**7.3**	**7.8**	**6.7**	**8.0**	**5.6**	**2.0**
2.4	**2.3**	**2.8**	**2.5**	**2.6**	**5.0**	**3.0**
0.7	**–3.0**	**4.3**	**3.4**	**1.7**	**5.0**	**3.0**
4.4	5.7	3.3	5.4	7.0	4.0	2.9
4.2	5.2	2.8	4.1	4.1	4.2	3.8
2.4	–1.8	6.0	5.8	3.4	7.8	3.3
..	..	4.4	..	..	4.4	2.8
1.3	5.1	–2.0	3.1	0.9	5.0	2.0
3.3	3.0	3.5	4.0	3.8	4.1	3.3
–0.6	–2.8	1.2	–0.2	–1.9	1.2	3.0
2.8	1.0	4.3	2.7	2.5	2.8	3.3
3.5	6.1	1.3	1.1	–1.6	3.5	2.5
–3.6	–17.1	8.1	6.8	1.5	11.3	2.6
–0.2	–5.0	4.6	3.4	0.4	6.3	3.0
–1.6	–4.5	1.9	3.1	2.9	3.3	2.5
1.8	–3.3	6.9	1.7	0.6	2.9	3.0
6.1	–3.8	10.3	4.3	0.4	6.0	2.7
1.6	0.0	2.9	0.4	0.3	0.4	3.2
0.8	–0.2	1.8	3.7	4.2	3.2	3.3
4.0	**7.1**	**1.5**	**1.8**	**3.5**	**0.5**	**3.0**
10.7	8.7	14.9	1.0	–0.1	3.2	2.8
4.5	7.6	1.9	2.6	2.1	3.0	3.2
3.7	2.4	4.7	4.7	5.9	3.6	2.7
2.5	12.5	–6.1	2.2	8.2	–2.9	2.9
6.0	7.1	4.9	6.1	7.2	5.0	2.6
1.4	0.5	2.2	–0.3	1.3	–1.7	2.7
8.7	16.0	–0.1	8.3	10.9	5.0	2.5
2.0	2.9	1.2	2.4	4.1	1.0	3.7
6.1	8.3	4.2	5.3	10.8	0.6	3.2
2.3	6.6	–1.5	–0.4	1.7	–2.1	3.8
..	0.1	0.5	..	–2.5	–1.3	5.4
..	..	10.4	..	..	7.3	2.2
1.2	3.8	–1.0	2.0	3.6	0.6	3.0
9.9	3.8	15.2	3.5	2.3	4.5	2.7
..	..	..	..	..	..	1.7

(table continues on next page)

TABLE A1.2 (continued)

	Agriculture		
	1981–93	*1981–86*	*1987–93*
Mali	3.4	3.0	3.8
Niger	..	3.4	..
Rwanda	0.2	0.2	0.1
São Tomé and Principe	−0.2	−0.7	0.5
Senegal[a]	2.1	4.1	0.4
Somalia	3.6	4.4	2.6
Sudan	1.2	4.7	−3.0
Togo	4.8	5.2	4.5
Zaire	2.3	2.5	2.0
East Asia and			
the Pacific	**5.3**	**6.9**	**3.9**
Cambodia	..	..	5.0
China	5.6	7.5	4.0
Kiribati	..	..	..
Lao PDR	..	..	..
Mongolia	1.0	3.8	−0.3
Myanmar	2.1	4.2	0.3
Solomon Islands	..	..	..
Tonga	..	..	..
Vanuatu	5.5	7.5	2.6
Viet Nam	4.4	3.1	4.7
Western Samoa	..	..	..
South Asia	**3.3**	**2.8**	**3.6**
Afghanistan	..	..	..
Bangladesh	2.9	3.9	2.0
Bhutan	4.2	6.0	2.7
India	3.2	2.3	3.9
Maldives	..	..	..
Nepal	4.3	5.2	3.6
Pakistan	4.4	5.3	3.6
Sri Lanka	2.6	4.2	1.3
Latin America and			
the Caribbean	**1.4**	**1.1**	**1.6**
Bolivia[a]	2.0	2.0	2.0
Guyana	1.3	0.7	1.9
Haiti	..	..	..

Industry			Services			Population
1981–93	1981–86	1987–93	1981–93	1981–86	1987–93	1981–93
4.6	7.2	2.3	0.3	–1.1	1.5	2.7
..	–3.0	..	..	–4.2	..	3.3
1.2	2.7	–0.2	4.7	13.0	–3.6	3.0
–0.5	–0.7	–0.2	–0.4	–0.7	0.2	2.2
2.8	2.1	3.5	2.9	3.8	2.0	3.0
0.0	2.7	–4.1	0.0	–0.4	0.4	3.1
4.2	5.6	2.6	2.0	0.1	4.2	2.7
–2.5	–2.6	–2.4	–4.2	–1.0	–7.0	3.5
1.2	3.1	–1.6	1.3	1.8	0.6	3.3
11.5	**10.1**	**12.8**	**10.1**	**12.2**	**8.3**	**1.5**
..	..	8.2	..	..	7.0	3.1
11.6	10.2	12.8	10.4	12.5	8.5	1.4
..	..	..	..	..	..	2.1
..	..	..	..	..	..	2.8
0.4	5.4	–1.7	2.9	8.6	0.4	2.8
3.4	3.7	3.1	2.0	3.4	0.8	2.2
..	..	..	..	..	..	3.0
..	..	..	..	..	..	–0.4
12.6	9.9	14.7	3.6	5.5	0.9	2.6
..	..	..	..	..	..	2.2
..	..	..	..	..	..	0.4
5.9	**6.4**	**5.5**	**6.1**	**6.6**	**5.8**	**2.2**
..	..	..	..	..	..	2.5
5.1	3.9	6.2	6.1	7.5	5.0	2.3
14.2	15.3	13.4	7.0	6.7	7.4	2.1
5.9	6.6	5.3	6.1	6.3	6.0	2.1
..	..	..	..	..	..	3.3
..	..	..	..	..	..	2.6
6.8	6.4	7.1	6.4	7.7	5.4	3.1
5.1	3.9	6.1	5.0	5.8	4.3	1.4
0.4	**–1.8**	**3.1**	**1.0**	**0.6**	**1.4**	**2.3**
–0.1	–5.9	6.9	0.6	–0.5	2.0	2.2
–1.5	–6.5	2.7	–0.9	–1.8	–0.2	0.4
..	..	..	..	..	..	1.9

(table continues on next page)

TABLE A1.2 (continued)

	Agriculture		
	1981–93	*1981–86*	*1987–93*
Honduras	3.0	1.5	4.2
Nicaragua	–0.4	–0.2	–0.6
Middle East and **North Africa**	..	..	..
Egypt, Arab Rep.	1.9	2.7	1.2
Yemen, Rep.	..	..	..
Eastern and **Central Europe**	**0.8**	**1.5**	**0.0**
Albania	0.3	2.7	–2.1
Armenia	–3.9	2.2	–11.1
Georgia	2.8	2.2	3.6
Kyrgyz Republic[a]	2.4	0.6	5.1
Macedonia, FYR[a]	..	..	..
Tajikistan	–2.3	–0.4	–5.2

a. Lower-middle-income economy but eligible for access to IDA resources.
Source: World Bank data.

Industry			Services			Population
1981–93	*1981–86*	*1987–93*	*1981–93*	*1981–86*	*1987–93*	*1981–93*
3.5	1.9	4.9	2.5	1.8	3.2	3.2
−1.7	1.1	−4.2	−0.4	0.3	−1.0	2.7
..	..	..	..	..	..	**2.7**
3.2	5.3	1.4	5.2	9.0	1.9	2.4
..	..	..	..	..	..	3.8
0.0	**4.1**	**−4.8**	**0.3**	**3.6**	**−3.7**	**1.7**
−6.1	3.0	−15.1	−0.5	2.5	−3.5	1.9
2.2	5.7	−2.1	2.7	4.7	0.4	1.4
−3.0	3.3	−10.6	−3.5	1.5	−9.4	0.6
5.4	4.1	7.3	7.2	8.3	5.4	1.8
..	..	..	..	..	..	..
3.2	3.8	2.4	5.5	6.9	3.4	2.9

TABLE A1.3 SELECTED SOCIAL INDICATORS IN LOW-INCOME
COUNTRIES

| | Percentage of age group enrolled in education | | | |
| | Primary | | Secondary | |
	1970	1990	1970	1990
Sub-Saharan Africa	**46**	**60**[a]	**6**	**18**
Angola	75	91	8	12
Benin	36	53[a]	5	11
Burkina Faso	13	29[a]	1	8
Burundi	30	50[a]	2	6
Cameroon[b]	89	76[a]	7	28
Cape Verde	66	95[a]	..	16
Central African Republic	64	56[a]	4	12
Chad	35	38[a]	2	7
Comoros	34	75	3	18
Congo[b]	..	..	..	..
Côte d'Ivoire	58	52[a]	9	22
Djibouti	..	37[a]	..	12
Equatorial Guinea	76	..	16	..
Ethiopia	16	28[a]	4	12
Gambia, The	24	54[a]	7	18
Ghana	64	77	14	38
Guinea	33	26[a]	13	9
Guinea-Bissau	39	45[a]	8	7
Kenya	58	95	9	29
Lesotho	87	70[a]	7	26
Liberia	56	..	10	..
Madagascar	90	64[a]	12	18
Malawi	..	50[a]	..	4
Mali	22	19[a]	5	7
Mauritania	14	51	2	16
Mozambique	47	45[a]	5	8
Niger	14	25[a]	1	7
Nigeria	37	72	4	20
Rwanda	68	67[a]	2	8
São Tomé and Principe	..	..	..	..
Senegal[b]	41	48[a]	10	16
Sierra Leone	34	48	8	16
Somalia	11	..	5	..

Adult literacy (percent)		Life expectancy at birth (years)		Infant mortality rate (per 1,000 live births)		Percentage of population with access to sanitation
Female 1992	Male 1992	1970	1992	1970	1992	1985–91
40	**63**	**43**	**51**	**144**	**100**	**31**
29	57	37	46	178	124	18
17	35	44	51	155	110	42
10	31	40	48	178	132	12
42	63	44	48	138	106	48
45	70	45	56	126	61	78
..	..	57	68	86	40	17
26	55	42	47	139	105	21
20	46	38	47	171	122	..
..	..	47	56	140	89	83
45	72	46	51	126	114	..
41	69	44	56	135	91	35
..	..	40	49	159	115	59
38	66	40	48	165	117	37
..	..	43	49	158	122	16
18	43	36	45	185	132	44
54	74	49	56	111	81	42
15	39	37	44	181	133	24
25	53	35	39	185	140	25
60	82	50	59	102	66	43
..	..	50	60	134	46	25
31	53	46	53	178	142	15
74	90	45	51	181	93	5
..	..	40	44	193	134	..
27	46	38	48	204	130	23
22	48	39	48	165	117	23
21	46	39	44	156	162	24
18	44	38	46	170	123	10
41	63	41	52	139	84	15
39	67	44	46	142	117	58
..	..	..	68	..	65	..
26	55	43	49	135	68	54
12	35	34	43	197	143	62
16	41	40	49	158	132	17

(table continues on next page)

TABLE A1.3 (continued)

| | Percentage of age group enrolled in education | | | |
| | Primary | | Secondary | |
	1970	1990	1970	1990
Sudan	38	50	7	22
Tanzania	34	51[a]	3	5
Togo	71	75[a]	7	23
Uganda	38	80	4	14
Zaire	88	58[a]	9	24
Zambia	90	82[a]	13	20
Zimbabwe	74	116	7	50
East Asia and the Pacific	**88**	**97**	**24**	**47**
Cambodia	30	..	8	..
China	89	98[a]	24	48
Kiribati	..	..	..	..
Lao PDR	53	59[a]	3	22
Mongolia	113	98	87	86
Myanmar	83	97	21	24
Solomon Islands	..	..	..	..
Tonga	..	..	..	..
Vanuatu	..	..	..	..
Viet Nam	..	103	..	33
Western Samoa	..	..	..	..
South Asia	**67**	**88**	**25**	**39**
Afghanistan	28	24	7	9
Bangladesh	54	69[a]	..	19
Bhutan	6	25	1	5
India	73	99	26	44
Maldives	..	..	..	..
Nepal	26	61	10	30
Pakistan	40	42	13	21
Sri Lanka	99	107	47	74
Latin America and the Caribbean	**81**	**69**	**22**	**32**
Bolivia[a]	76	82[a]	24	34
Guyana	98	112	55	58
Haiti	..	26[a]	..	22

Adult literacy (percent)		Life expectancy at birth (years)		Infant mortality rate (per 1,000 live births)		Percentage of population with access to sanitation
Female 1992	Male 1992	1970	1992	1970	1992	1985–91
13	45	42	52	149	99	70
..	..	46	51	132	92	66
33	59	44	55	134	85	21
37	65	50	43	109	122	31
63	86	45	52	128	91	25
67	83	46	48	106	107	43
61	76	51	60	96	47	42
69	**92**	**61**	**69**	**72**	**33**	**90**
24	52	..	58	105	60	15
68	92	62	69	69	31	97
..	..	42	51	161	116	..
..	..	40	51	146	97	24
..	..	51	60	121	72	73
72	90	53	64	102	60	36
..	..	..	62	..	44	..
..	..	..	68	..	21	..
..	..	..	63	..	45	46
84	93	55	67	104	36	18
..	..	..	66	..	25	..
33	**61**	**49**	**60**	**138**	**83**	**18**
15	48	37	43	198	162	..
23	49	45	55	140	91	32
26	55	40	48	182	129	9
35	64	49	61	137	79	15
..	..	51	62	119	55	28
14	39	42	54	157	99	8
22	49	48	59	142	95	24
85	94	65	72	53	18	60
65	**76**	**50**	**61**	**131**	**72**	**45**
72	86	46	60	153	82	35
96	99	60	65	80	48	90
49	61	48	55	141	93	27

(table continues on next page)

TABLE A1.3 (continued)

| | Percentage of age group enrolled in education | | | |
| | Primary | | Secondary | |
	1970	1990	1970	1990
Honduras	87	93[a]	14	31
Nicaragua	80	76[a]	18	40
Middle East and North Africa	**64**	**97**	**30**	**71**
Egypt, Arab Rep.	72	101	35	81
Yemen, Rep.	22	79	3	23
Middle-income Sub-Saharan Africa	**83**	**70**	**17**	**36**
Botswana	65	96[a]	7	43
Gabon	85	..	8	..
Mauritius	94	92[a]	30	53
Namibia	..	81[a]	..	41
Seychelles	..	..	..	..
Swaziland	87	85[a]	18	47
Middle-income East Asia and Pacific (high performing)	**85**	**98**	**21**	**49**
Indonesia	80	98[a]	16	45
Korea, Rep.	103	100[a]	42	87
Malaysia	87	93	34	56
Thailand	83	99	17	33

a. Net enrollment ratio.
b. Lower-middle-income economy but eligible for access to IDA resources.
Source: World Bank data.

Adult literacy (percent)		Life expectancy at birth (years)		Infant mortality rate (per 1,000 live births)		Percentage of population with access to sanitation
Female 1992	Male 1992	1970	1992	1970	1992	1985–91
73	78	53	66	110	49	67
..	..	54	67	106	56	52
34	64	50	60	161	66	54
35	66	51	62	158	57	51
28	56	42	53	175	106	68
38	49	51	62	106	59	37
66	85	50	68	101	35	42
50	76	44	54	138	94	..
75	85	62	70	60	18	98
..	..	48	59	118	57	15
..	..	..	71	..	16	65
..	..	46	57	145	108	40
82	93	52	64	95	48	61
77	91	47	60	118	66	44
95	99	60	71	51	13	100
72	89	62	71	45	14	94
92	96	58	69	73	26	74

TABLE A1.4 GROSS DOMESTIC INVESTMENT AND GROSS DOMESTIC SAVINGS
(percentage of GDP)

	Gross domestic investment			Gross domestic savings		
	1981–93	*1981–86*	*1987–93*	*1981–93*	*1981–86*	*1987–93*
Low-income countries	**25.9**	**24.1**	**27.3**	**21.2**	**20.5**	**23.2**
Sub-Saharan Africa	**16.3**	**16.6**	**16.5**	**12.1**	**11.5**	**12.5**
Reforming countries	**16.8**	**15.6**	**17.9**	**13.4**	**11.8**	**14.9**
Burundi	15.9	16.4	15.5	0.8	4.1	–2.0
Gambia, The	18.9	19.0	18.8	6.4	6.2	6.7
Ghana	10.7	6.3	14.4	5.5	5.5	5.4
Guinea	16.0	..	16.3	13.9	..	13.4
Guinea-Bissau	28.5	27.2	29.6	–7.3	–4.7	–9.6
Kenya	22.5	23.1	21.9	19.9	20.7	19.1
Madagascar	10.7	9.1	12.1	3.5	2.0	4.9
Malawi	17.7	17.6	17.9	10.1	13.3	7.3
Mauritania	27.1	31.9	23.0	7.4	3.0	11.2
Mozambique	27.1	16.6	36.1	–9.0	–4.2	–13.1
Nigeria	15.2	15.3	15.1	17.4	13.3	21.6
Sierra Leone	12.3	13.5	11.2	7.9	7.0	8.7
Tanzania	27.7	18.3	37.1	7.3	9.7	5.0
Uganda	10.4	7.3	13.0	1.7	2.9	0.6
Zambia	15.1	17.2	13.3	13.9	14.1	13.8
Zimbabwe	20.6	19.6	21.6	19.6	17.9	21.1
Other African countries	**15.9**	**17.4**	**15.0**	**10.9**	**11.3**	**10.1**
Angola	15.5	..	14.2	22.3	..	24.1
Benin	14.7	16.0	13.6	2.4	0.8	3.8
Burkina Faso	20.5	20.0	21.0	–0.8	–4.9	2.6
Cameroon[a]	20.8	24.8	17.4	21.5	29.1	15.0
Cape Verde	43.8	54.0	33.6	–3.9	–5.4	–2.4
Central African Republic	11.4	11.0	11.7	–0.8	–2.0	0.2
Chad	7.7	5.9	8.9	–13.3	–11.6	–14.5
Comoros	25.0	31.7	19.2	–3.3	–4.1	–2.7
Congo[a]	27.3	39.4	17.0	26.5	35.7	18.5
Côte d'Ivoire	13.6	17.1	10.6	18.1	21.7	15.1
Djibouti	18.3	22.4	16.5	–7.0	–3.5	–8.5
Equatorial Guinea	22.0	..	25.6	–8.7	..	–9.5
Ethiopia	12.8	12.4	13.2	3.1	3.0	3.2

TABLE A1.4 (continued)

	Gross domestic investment			Gross domestic savings		
	1981–93	*1981–86*	*1987–93*	*1981–93*	*1981–86*	*1987–93*
Lesotho	54.7	43.9	63.9	−64.7	−80.9	−50.7
Liberia	11.8	11.8	..	14.7	14.7	..
Mali	19.8	17.2	22.0	1.2	−3.5	5.2
Niger	11.9	13.9	10.1	6.7	6.1	7.2
Rwanda	15.1	15.6	14.7	4.7	6.1	3.4
São Tomé and Principe	41.2	37.6	44.4	−18.8	−17.6	−19.9
Senegal[a]	12.2	11.3	12.9	3.5	−0.4	6.9
Somalia	26.2	26.4	25.8	−6.2	−9.7	−1.0
Sudan	14.1	14.1	14.1	4.8	3.6	6.2
Togo	23.5	25.3	21.9	15.5	18.8	12.7
Zaire	11.9	10.7	14.4	10.7	10.2	11.9
East Asia and the Pacific	**34.0**	**31.4**	**36.4**	**29.2**	**31.0**	**32.7**
China	35.1	32.4	37.5	35.9	32.2	39.0
Other East Asia and the Pacific	**16.2**	**17.1**	**15.9**	**10.2**	**11.5**	**10.6**
Cambodia	..	..	..	..	..	..
Kiribati	35.8	35.8	..	−48.9	−48.9	..
Lao PDR	10.2	6.7	12.3	−0.3	2.3	−1.9
Mongolia	45.2	58.8	33.6	19.5	26.9	13.1
Myanmar	15.3	17.8	12.8	12.1	12.9	11.2
Solomon Islands	30.2	29.5	31.0	8.9	9.8	7.8
Tonga	..	25.3	..	..	−9.4	..
Vanuatu	32.4	18.7	36.7	9.4	6.7	8.6
Viet Nam	16.4	..	16.5	10.1	..	10.8
Western Samoa	32.1	30.0	34.1	−8.3	−8.4	−8.2
South Asia	**23.0**	**22.1**	**23.7**	**19.4**	**17.8**	**20.8**
India	24.1	23.0	25.1	21.8	20.3	23.1
Other South Asia	**18.1**	**18.2**	**17.9**	**9.0**	**7.0**	**10.8**
Afghanistan	..	..	..	..	..	..
Bangladesh	13.1	13.7	12.6	3.2	2.0	4.3
Bhutan	37.2	40.2	34.3	12.5	9.9	15.0
Maldives	..	..	..	..	..	..
Nepal	20.4	19.5	21.2	11.7	11.8	11.6
Pakistan	19.0	18.7	19.2	10.9	8.0	13.4
Sri Lanka	24.6	26.5	23.0	13.4	13.4	13.5

(table continues on next page)

TABLE A1.4 (continued)

	Gross domestic investment			Gross domestic savings		
	1981–93	*1981–86*	*1987–93*	*1981–93*	*1981–86*	*1987–93*
Latin America and the Caribbean	**16.6**	**16.1**	**18.1**	**8.0**	**10.1**	**7.3**
Bolivia[a]	11.9	10.3	13.2	8.7	10.8	6.9
Guyana	33.3	30.2	36.0	21.1	15.6	25.8
Haiti	14.2	15.5	12.2	4.9	5.7	3.8
Honduras	17.8	16.3	22.6	13.1	11.6	17.2
Nicaragua	20.9	21.2	20.7	1.8	9.8	−5.0
Middle East and North Africa	..	..	..	..	..	..
Egypt, Arab Republic	24.0	27.7	20.8	10.4	14.9	6.5
Yemen, Republic	19.0	..	19.3	−4.0	..	−1.0
Eastern and Central Europe	**26.4**	**27.3**	**25.3**	**21.6**	**27.0**	**16.0**
Albania	28.3	34.1	22.4	17.8	32.4	3.3
Armenia	26.3	26.6	26.0	20.1	32.5	9.5
Georgia	24.0	24.8	22.9	25.4	27.6	22.2
Kyrgyz Republic[a]	30.8	30.9	30.6	18.2	19.3	16.9
Macedonia, FYR[a]	..	..	..	..	..	..
Tajikistan	27.7	29.3	25.8	17.7	20.2	14.7

a. Lower-middle-income economy but eligible for access to IDA resources.
Source: World Bank data.

Selected bibliography

General

International Finance Corporation. 1994. "IFC's Operations in Africa." Washington, D.C.

Jegathesan, J. 1995. "Investment Environment in Developing Economies in the Context of Foreign Direct Investments." Paper presented at a seminar on policies for growth in Africa, Paris, February 13–14.

Kinoshita, Toshihiko. 1995. "How to Facilitate Private Investment in Africa: Based on the Experiences in East Asian Economic Success." Paper presented at a seminar on policies for growth in Africa, Paris, February 13–14.

Mosley, Paul, Jane Harrigan, and John Toye. 1991. *Aid and Power: The World Bank and Policy-Based Lending*. New York: Routledge.

Naim, Moises. 1993. *Paper Tigers and Minotaurs: The Politics of Venezuela's Economic Reforms*. Washington, D.C.: Carnegie Endowment for International Peace.

OECD (Organization for Economic Cooperation and Development). 1994. "Development Assistance Committee Orientations for Development Cooperation in Support of Private Sector Development." DCD/DAC (94) 20. Paris.

———. 1994. "Private Sector Development: Implications for Aid." DCD/DAC (94) 20. Paris.

World Bank. 1987. "The World Bank's Role in Promoting the Private Sector." Report M87-1185. Washington, D.C.

———. 1988. *World Development Report 1988: Public Finance in Development*. New York: Oxford University Press.

———. 1989. "Private Sector Development Action Program." Report R89-9, IDA/R89-6, IFC/R89-5. Washington, D.C.

————. 1990. *World Development Report 1990: Poverty.* New York: Oxford University Press.

————. 1991a. *Developing the Private Sector: The World Bank's Experience and Approach.* Washington, D.C.

————. 1991b. *Private Sector Development: Strengthening the Bank Group Effort.* Report R91-79, IDA/R91-52, IFC/R91-60. Washington, D.C.

————. 1991c. *World Development Report 1991: The Challenge of Development.* New York: Oxford University Press.

————. 1993a. *The East Asian Miracle: Economic Growth and Public Policy.* A World Bank Policy Research Report. New York: Oxford University Press.

————. 1993b. *Private Sector Development: A Progress Report.* Washington, D.C.

————. 1994. *Adjustment in Africa: Reforms, Results, and the Road Ahead.* A World Bank Policy Research Report. New York: Oxford University Press.

————. 1995. *Bureaucrats in Business: The Economics and Politics of Government Ownership.* A World Bank Policy Research Report. Washington, D.C.

Chapter 1: From state to market—uneven progress

Binswanger, Hans. 1990. "The Policy Response of Agriculture." In Stanley Fischer and Dennis de Tray, eds., *Proceedings of the World Bank Annual Conference on Development Economics 1989.* Washington, D.C.: World Bank.

Chen, Shaohua, Martin Ravallion, and Gaurav Datt. 1993. "Is Poverty Increasing in the Developing World?" Policy Research Working Paper 1146. World Bank, Washington, D.C.

"A Continent Discovered: Whether the Government Can Stay on the Chinese Economic Tiger." *Financial Times,* November 4, 1994.

"Financial Times Survey: China." *Financial Times,* November 7, 1994.

GATT (General Agreement on Trade and Tariffs). 1993. "International Trade 1993: Statistics." Geneva.

International Monetary Fund. Various years. *Government Finance Statistics Yearbook.* Washington D.C.

————. Various years. *International Financial Statistics.* Washington D.C.

Lall, Sanjaya. 1993. "Trade Policies for Development: A Policy Prescription for Africa." *Development Policy Review* 11 (1).

Lardy, Nicholas. 1994. *China in the World Economy.* Washington, D.C.: Institute of International Economics.

Miller, Robert, and Mariusz A. Sumlinski. 1994. "Trends in Private Investment in Developing Countries: Statistics for 1970–92." International Finance Corporation Discussion Paper 20. Washington, D.C.

Schloss, Miguel. 1993. "Do Petroleum Procurement and Trade Matter? The Case of Sub-Saharan Africa." *Finance and Development* 30 (1).

World Bank. 1989. *Sub-Saharan Africa: From Crisis to Sustainable Growth: A Long-Term Perspective Study.* Washington, D.C.

———. 1992. *African Development Indicators.* Washington D.C.

———. 1994. *Social Indicators of Development.* Baltimore: Johns Hopkins University Press.

———. 1994. *World Tables.* Baltimore: Johns Hopkins University Press.

———. 1995. "A Continent in Transition: Sub-Saharan Africa in the Mid-1990s." Washington, D.C.

Chapter 2: Establishing an attractive business environment—agile firms, agile institutions

Bachmann, Heinz, and Ken Kwaku, eds. 1994. "MIGA Roundtable on Foreign Direct Investment in Africa: Proceedings and Lessons." Policy and Advisory Services Research Paper Series, Multilateral Investment Guarantee Agency, Washington, D.C.

Bennell, Paul. 1995. "British Manufacturing Investment in Sub-Saharan Africa: Corporate Response During Structural Adjustment." Working Paper 13. University of Sussex, Institute of Development Studies, Brighton, U.K.

Biggs, Tyler, G. Moody, and J-M van Leeuwen. 1994. *Africa Can Compete! Export Opportunities and Challenges for Garments and Home Products in the U.S. Market.* World Bank Discussion Paper 242. Washington, D.C.

European Roundtable of Industrialists. 1993. "European Industry: A Partner of the Developing World." Brussels.

Foreign Investment Advisory Service. 1994. "The Impact of the Foreign Investment Advisory Service." World Bank, Washington, D.C.

Gopal, Mohan Gopalan. 1993. "A Critique of the Legal Response to the Problems of Debt Recovery and Collateral Security." World Bank, Legal Department, Washington, D.C.

Government of India. 1994. *Economic Survey, 1993–94.* New Delhi: Government of India Press.

Grey, Cheryl W. 1993. *Evolving Legal Frameworks for Private Sector Development in Central and Eastern Europe.* World Bank Discussion Paper 209. Washington, D.C.

Institutional Investor. Various issues.

International Finance Corporation. 1993. "Report on the Activities of the African Enterprise Fund." Washington, D.C.

———. 1994. *Lessons from Successful Investments in Sub-Saharan Africa.* Report M94-86. Washington, D.C.

International Finance Corporation and Multilateral Investment Guarantee Agency. 1991. *The Impact of the Foreign Investment Advisory Service on Investment Policies in Developing Countries.* Report IFC/M91-25, MIGA/M91-12. World Bank, Washington, D.C.

Khatkhate, Deena R. 1992. *The Regulatory Impediments to the Private Industrial Sector Development in Asia: A Comparative Study.* World Bank Discussion Paper 177. Washington, D.C.

Middleton, John, Adrian Ziderman, and Arvil Van Adams. 1993. *Skills for Productivity: Vocational Education and Training in Developing Countries.* New York: Oxford University Press.

Rhee, Yung Whee, and Therese Belot. 1989. "Export Catalysts in Low-Income Countries: Preliminary Findings from a Review of Export Success Stories in Eleven Developing Countries." Industry and Energy Department Working Paper Series, Industry Paper 5. World Bank, Washington, D.C.

Sader, Frank. 1993. "Privatizations and Foreign Investment in the Developing World: 1988–92." World Bank, International Economics Department, Washington, D.C.

Shihata, Ibrahim F. I. 1993. "Judicial Reform in Developing Countries and the Role of the World Bank." Paper presented at a seminar on justice in Latin America and the Caribbean. San Jose, Costa Rica.

Umali-Deininger, Dina L., Clare Narrod, and Klaus Deininger. 1994. "Private Sector Development in Agriculture: Constraints, Opportunities, and New Approaches." World Bank, Agricultural Policies Division, Washington, D.C.

Webb, Douglas A. 1994. "Private Sector Development in Low-Income Countries—A Legal Perspective." World Bank, Legal Department, Legal Reform and Private Sector Development Unit, Washington, D.C.

World Bank. 1992a. *Law, Legal Procedure, and the Economic Value of Collateral: The Case of Bolivia.* Report 10627-BO. Washington, D.C.

————. 1992b. *Strategy for African Mining.* World Bank Technical Paper 181. Industry and Energy Department, Mining Unit. Washington, D.C.

————. 1994a. "Enhancing Africa's Capacity for Private Investment Promotion and Image-Building." Washington D.C.

————. 1994b. "Industrial Sector Reorientation in East Africa: The Experience in Kenya, Malawi, Tanzania, and Zambia." Operations Evaluation Department, Washington, D.C.

————. 1994c. "Legal Technical Assistance: Initial Lessons Learned." Legal Department, Washington, D.C.

————. 1994d. *World Debt Tables 1993–94.* Washington, D.C.

————. 1994e. *World Development Report 1994: Infrastructure for Development.* New York: Oxford University Press.

Chapter 3: Reforming public enterprises— farther and faster

Bell, Stuart. 1995. *Sharing the Wealth: Privatization through Broad-Based Ownership Strategies.* World Bank Discussion Paper 285. Washington, D.C.

Berg, Elliot. 1994. "Privatization in Sub-Saharan Africa." *Development Alternatives Incorporated.*

EdF International. 1992. "Power Utility Management by Performance Contracting." Seminar presented at the World Bank, Washington, D.C, May 19.

Ewing, Andrew, and Susan Goldmark. 1994. "Privatization by Capitalization: The Case of Bolivia." *FPD Note* 31. World Bank, Washington, D.C.

Galal, Ahmed, Leroy Jones, Pankaj Tardon, and Ingo Vogelsang. 1994. *Welfare Consequences of Selling Public Enterprises: An Empirical Analysis.* New York: Oxford University Press.

International Finance Corporation. 1994. *Financing Private Infrastructure Projects: Emerging Trends from IFC's Experience.* Washington, D.C.

Kessides, Christine. 1993. *Institutional Options for the Provision of Infrastructure.* World Bank Discussion Paper 212. Washington, D.C.

Kikeri, Sunita, John Nellis, and Mary Shirley. 1992. *Privatization: The Lessons of Experience.* Washington D.C.: World Bank.

Klein, Michael, and Neil D. Roger. 1994. "Back to the Future: The Potential *in Infrastructure Privatization." In Richard O'Brien, ed., Finance and the International Economy* 8. Oxford: Oxford University Press

MacMurray, Trevor, and Jonathan Woetzel. 1994. "The Challenge Facing China's State-Owned Enterprises." *McKinsey Quarterly* 2.

Sherif, Khaled. 1993. "Regional Study on Public Enterprise Reform and Privatization in Africa." World Bank, Africa Technical Department, Washington, D.C.

Triche, Thelma. 1992. "Private Sector Participation in Urban Water Supply: Issues, Implications, and Examples." INUWS Note. World Bank, Washington, D.C.

World Bank. 1992. "World Bank Structural and Sectoral Adjustment Operations: The Second OED Overview." Operations Evaluation Department. Washington, D.C.

———. 1994. "China: Meeting the Challenge of Enterprise Reform." China and Mongolia Department, Industry and Energy Operations Division. Washington, D.C.

————. 1995. *Bureaucrats in Business: The Economics and Politics of Government Ownership.* A World Bank Policy Research Report. Washingon, D.C.

Chapter 4: Building robust financial systems— difficult but pressing

Christen, Robert Peck, Elisabeth Rhyne, and Robert C. Vogel. 1994. "Maximizing the Outreach of Microenterprise Finance: The Emerging Lessons of Successful Programs." IMCC, Consulting Assistance for Economic Reform Paper.

de Juan, Aristobulo. 1991. "Does Bank Insolvency Matter? What to do about it?" In Philippe Callier, ed., *Financial Systems and Development in Africa.* World Bank: Washington, D.C.

Larrain, Mauricio. 1989. "How the 1981-83 Chilean Banking Crisis was Handled" Policy, Planning, and Research Working Paper 300. World Bank, Washington, D.C.

Popiel, Paul. 1994. *Financial Systems in Africa: A Comparative Study.* World Bank Discussion Paper 260. Washington, D.C.

Rhyne, Elizabeth, and Linda Rotblatt. 1994. "What Makes Them Tick? Exploring the Anatomy of Major Microenterprise Finance Organizations." ACCION International Monograph Series 9. Washington, D.C.

Webster, Leila. 1994. "Lending for Microenterprises—A Review of the World Bank's Portfolio." *FPD Note 23.* World Bank, Washington, D.C.

World Bank. 1989. *World Development Report 1989: Financial Systems and Development.* New York: Oxford University Press.

————. 1994. *Adjustment in Africa: Reforms, Results, and the Road Ahead.* A World Bank Policy Research Report. New York: Oxford University Press.

————. 1995. *Bureaucrats in Business: The Economics and Politics of Government Ownership.* A World Bank Policy Research Report. Washington, D.C.

Yaron, Jacob. 1992. *Successful Rural Finance Institutions.* World Bank Discussion Paper 150. Washington, D.C.

Yusuf, Shahid. 1994. "China's Collective and Private Enterprises: Growth and Its Financing." In Gerard Caprio, David Folkerts-Landau, and Timothy D. Lane, eds., *Building Sound Finance in Emerging Market Economies.* Washington, D.C.: International Monetary Fund.